CONQUERING THE FEAR PANDEMIC

MIKE HENDRICK

CONQUERING THE FEAR PANDEMIC

MIKE HENDRICK

CONQUERING THE FEAR PANDEMIC

Copyright © 2020 by Mike Hendrick
First Edition: December 2020
Published by: Mike Hendrick
E-Mail: thefearpandemicbook@gmail.com

Cover and Layout Design: Theodore Dones, Divine Design Studio, Crestwood, Kentucky www.divinedesignstudio.org

Interior Formatting: Deborah G. Hunter, Hunter Entertainment Network, Colorado Springs, Colorado www.hunter-ent-net.com

Back Photo: Tony Fehr, Rising Son Photography, Calgary, Alberta
https://risingsonphotography.com/

Edited by Cheryl Mark & Deborah G. Hunter

All rights reserved: No part of this publication may be reproduced, stored, in a retrieval system, or transmitted in any form or by any means – electronic, mechanical, digital, photocopy, recording, or any other – without the expressed prior permission by the author or publisher. The opinion and views expressed in this book are solely of the author.

This book contains some personal stories from the author's life. It reflects the author's present recollections of experiences over time. Some characteristics have been changed, some events have been compressed, and some dialogue has been recreated.

The content of this book is also for informational purposes only and is not intended to diagnose, treat, cure, or prevent any condition or disease. You understand that this book is not intended as a substitute for consultation with a licensed practitioner. Please consult with your own practitioner or specialist regarding the suggestions and recommendations made in this book. The use of this book implies your acceptance of this disclaimer.

All scripture is quoted from: Amplified Bible Classic Edition (AMPC),
English Standard Version (ESV), and New International Version 1984 (NIV)

"Scripture quotations taken from the Amplified® Bible Classic, Copyright © 1954, 1958, 1962, 1964, 1965, 1987 by The Lockman Foundation Used by permission." (www.Lockman.org)

"Scripture quotations are from The Holy Bible, English Standard Version® (ESV®), copyright © 2001 by Crossway, a publishing ministry of Good News Publishers. Used by permission. All rights reserved."

Scripture taken from the HOLY BIBLE, NEW INTERNATIONAL VERSION®. Copyright © 1973, 1978, 1984 Biblica. Used by permission of Zondervan. All rights reserved. The "NIV" and "New International Version" trademarks are registered in the United States Patent and Trademark Office by Biblica. Use of either trademark requires the permission of Biblica.

ISBN: 9798558967500

Dedication

This book is dedicated to the following:

My parents Gaylene and Gary Hendrick raised me in the Christian faith while they prayed and supported me in my battles of fear. They may not always have understood the process I was walking through or why I was facing certain challenges, but their faith in God and love for me has kept me anchored during my deepest trials.

Pastor Kenn and Cheryl Gill, my spiritual father and mother in faith and pastors in my life for over 28 years in Calgary. They have loved me as a son and have been spiritual counsel to me since I was 14 years old. You helped me walk through my healing journey. Thank you for all your generosity and for the many years of unconditional love. Walking with you as a spiritual son has been a joy and an honor. I am thankful for the countless enriching conversations on faith over the years. You encourage me continually to keep short accounts with people and give God my *yes*, no matter what He asks of me.

Cheryl and Archie Mark have believed in me for over 25 years. They recognized and shaped my prophetic calling. They have had countless discussions on the prophetic process and have given me many resources. Every time they would release me to minister, it built confidence in me that I could hear the voice of God. They allowed key ministers to speak over my destiny. Thank you for your assistance in editing the manuscript.

Pastor Bryan and Avis Logan and the congregation of *Life Connexion*, Westlock, Alberta for giving me many opportunities to minister to your congregation. Their congregation's love for me has been a major part of my healing journey. I joyfully share about the love and support I so tangibly feel from you everywhere I travel.

Pastor Richard Gazowsky and family of *A Place to Meet Jesus Church*, San Francisco, California. The twenty-year relationship with your family and church has been special. You saw God's hand on me when I was just being shaped in secret to now. Thank you for the many times of fellowship in San Francisco. You inspired me to write after reading your books. Your family has supported and prayed for me faithfully. Your example encourages me to step out and follow the voice of God, no matter the outcome.

Dr. Don Hughes: Thank you for letting me minister with you in Northern Canada and helping me with the connections I needed to facilitate the writing of this book. You saw my prophetic calling and made room for it in your meetings.

To Graham and Sherry Bretherick, your gift of counseling has been a precious, timely gift. You helped me heal from the troubled past of my childhood and move into a new dimension of freedom as an adult. You made it easy to discuss some of the deepest battles I faced. This book would never been a reality if you had not helped.

Endorsements

Mike Hendrick is a breed apart. He has come out of his own wilderness, transparently revealing his past struggles and his road to overcoming them. Mike has conquered his fears and now pens his insight and revelation to the Church and the world. His life and seasons have all been preparation "for such a time as this." We have ministered together on several occasions and I have found his prophetic gifting to be very accurate. He is humble, a servant, and a present-day oracle of God. His insight into the subject of fear and the timely release of this manuscript will help many break free of fear's tormenting grip. Read it, read it again, get an extra copy, and give it to someone that has the same struggles. Many victories and testimonials will be experienced, lived out, and seen by many as the result of this book's release. Great job Prophet, your friend and co-laborer in His Kingdom.

Dr. Don Hughes
Apostolic Leader and Lead Instructor
REV House School of Ministry
Tulsa, Oklahoma

Many believers never reach their God-given destiny because of fear. Mike addresses how to overcome this, not just in theory, but in openness and vulnerability in sharing his own story. The truths will help to move you from fear to faith!

Tony Fitzgerald
Apostolic Team Leader, Church of the Nations
Richmond, Virginia

In his book, "Conquering the Fear Pandemic," Mike shares his life journey with all of his heart and soul. Press in … you will discover a refreshingly vulnerable testimony landing on the foundation of God's timeless principles. For all who struggle with fear and overcoming their past, this book will surprise you with tangible ways to rise above and soar like an eagle!

Mark Eshleman
Senior Pastor, Ignited Church
Drayton Valley, Alberta

"The power of story" is an increasingly popular phrase used to express the impact of hearing, and of telling, an individual's unique experiences. In this book, my friend Mike effectively weaves together his own story with the Greatest Story Ever Told (The Gospel of Jesus). We travel with him through difficulties, pain, and confusion into victories, healing, and revelation, and on into the continuing journey of discovering the heart of Father God for each and every one of us. I invite you, the reader, to open your soul and be challenged and encouraged by these words to press into the plans of the Lord to give you hope and a future!

Russ Kline
International Prophetic Minister, Shatter the Darkness Ministries
Hampton, Virginia

I was really blessed and impressed by Mike's book entitled: "Conquering the Fear Pandemic." He has been through a lot in life, but he has refused to give in to all the lies he has been told and all the shaming and bullying he has been through. Way to go, Mike! You are a model of encouragement for others who have struggled with how they've been treated in life. Mike has some excellent wisdom and practical advice for people who have wrestled with various issues while growing up. His personal stories and triumphs encourage faith in the reader to turn to Jesus for a way out of seemingly impossible situations.

I am blessed by Mike's perseverance and doggedness to keep on "keeping on" in the face of difficult challenges. He uses real wisdom in discussing the challenges that COVID-19 has thrust upon our society and the world. I also love the courage that Mike displayed in confronting his fear, shame, and bullying from his junior high years. As I was reading his manuscript, I found myself cheering for Mike, thankful that he faced his fears and experienced significant growth because of his courage. His stories of redemption and transformation are very inspiring.

Having written a book myself on dealing with anger through forgiveness, I was especially impressed with Mike's personal, theological, and practical understanding of forgiveness. For me, forgiveness is one of the most powerful forces in life and Mike is a living demonstration of how forgiveness set him free to walk in a new way of life and also helped him overcome his fear.

Mike's book and his story will surely bring encouragement and hope to many others. Mike, I'm so glad you took on the challenge and put pen to paper, recording your life experiences and how Jesus helped you be an overcomer.

Graham Bretherick
Registered Psychologist, Run Free Counselling Centre
Lethbridge, Alberta

Years ago, we heard Mike share publicly; his words carried clarity and weight. His story, "Conquering the Fear Pandemic," also carries undeniable clarity and weight. Mike's life purpose is to exhort, encourage, and comfort as a prophetic voice to his generation. His experience and wisdom shared in his "blast of light" story, unveils how he ran courageously towards the potentially crippling abuse foundations in his life and worked with Jesus Christ, His Lord, to pole-vault high strongholds of fear. We honor you Mike for your vulnerability and honesty. Thank you. Your story undoes us with God's goodness. We honor you in your pursuit of The Truth through your lifestyle of fasting and prayer, study of God's Word, and loving His Bride, the Church. You have been accelerated by perseverance in seeking God's help from strategic apostolic and prophetic men and women, whom you honor well. May God give you supernatural increase to be His voice declaring God's way, God's will, and God's living Word.

Archie and Cheryl Mark
Founders, Arise Hub
Calgary, Alberta

Facing fear, rejection, and abuse, Mike shares his real and raw story while providing healing and freedom insights. Many people will discover hope and begin their recovery journey through his book, "Conquering the Fear Pandemic."

Glenn Shaffer
Apostolic Teams International
Claremore, Oklahoma

Mike Hendrick is a very special man, who is passionate for the Lord. I have known Mike as a man of faith. He has attended my meetings and conferences for many years. He is passionate about God's people and his prophetic words are accurate. Mike's desire is for the Lord and he is writing this book from a place of love. I've seen him conquer fear by stepping out in faith, in both business and ministry.

Mike is qualified to write a book about fear. For he has not only experienced its reality, but also conquered it. He will help you overcome fear in your life and help you discover God's truth that sets you free. I recommend this man and the book, and hope you get to meet Mike. This book will help you dismantle fear, its energy, and its power that has currently flooded the whole world. In this book, you will learn to walk in God's boldness, and you will find hope and peace as you read about God's insight through Mike's writing and life story. I encourage you to pick up this book and live a life of freedom for you and your family.

Dr. Gershom Sikaala
His Presence Fire Ministries and personal friend of author
Los Angeles, California

As you read this book," Conquering the Fear Pandemic," you will get a glimpse into Mike's journey of overcoming. My husband and I and our congregation have walked with Mike for the last eight years, watching as the Lord's love continues to heal and mature him. Through his intimate relationship with Father God, and walking closely as a spiritual son to Kenn Gill, he is blossoming into his call as a prophet who carries a rich grasp of the Word of God. Whether he preaches or ministers prophetically to our people, his words spoken have not returned void. Be prepared to be in awe of God's grace, love, and empowerment demonstrated through Mike's life journey.

Avis Logan
Co-Pastor, Life Connexion Church
Westlock, Alberta

In walking with Mike Hendrick for the last number of years, I have observed a deep ripening of character and clarity of thought. As an avid student of the scriptures, Mike has sharpened his gift to hear God's heart in a timely fashion. His perseverance through inordinate challenges have served to fashion Mike to emerge as a capable herald of God's truth in bewildering times. With candid transparency and testimony of God's grace, Mike offers us a timely exhortation to walk ahead in God's peace and healing.

Rev. Dr. Bryan A. Logan
Senior Pastor, Life Connexion Church
Westlock, Alberta

As I read the book, I began to feel faith stirring inside of me, a readiness to step out into areas of the unknown that Father had once called me to. Fear can hold you captive and delay all that God has in store for you. As Mike takes you on his personal journey of healing, you will meet God, the Father. "Conquering the Fear Pandemic" will encourage you to find the confidence to embrace His love and the healing power of His Word. Step out of your comfort zone and take the Father's hand as He takes you on a journey of His perfect love.

Misty Tarkington
School teacher and friend of author
Visalia, California

Having known Mike Hendrick for over five years, I have observed that he puts effort and excellence to whatever he does. This book is no different. I have thoroughly enjoyed reading it and believe it will aid many to overcome hidden fear in their lives that prevented them from moving forward and becoming everything they have been destined for. His peculiar, unique personality and life experiences have shaped him into who he is today. I admire his loyalty to both God and others, and consider it an honor to call him my friend.

Walter Viveiros
Founder and CEO, Hospitality Environments
Weeki Wachee, Florida

Table of Contents

Foreword 1

Chapter 1: A Gentle Whisper 5

Chapter 2: Exploring the Labyrinth of Fear................................... 13

Chapter 3: COVID-19 27

Chapter 4: The Power of Words 33

Chapter 5: Shame's Crippling Effects... 43

Chapter 6: Abuse & Bullying 57

Chapter 7: Rejections 69

Chapter 8: Perfectionism... 83

Chapter 9: The Power of Forgiveness 95

Chapter 10: All You Need is Love... 107

Chapter 11: The Power of Praise & Worship 119

Chapter 12: Standing on the Promises 129

Chapter 13: One Small Step.. 147

Bibliography 151

Foreword

Watching someone grow, mature, develop, and blossom has to be one of the highlights of leading the people of God.

Our family has known and loved Michael for almost three decades. We met him while pastoring a church his family chose to attend when they moved to Calgary. He was an eager junior-higher wanting to know and serve God with all his heart. I noted that Mike also gravitated to 'spiritual leaders' holding them in the highest regard and desiring to spend time with them, and serve them however he could. We, as a family, have been the recipient of that love and honor in an un-interruptive fashion over this same time period.

From time to time over the years, I would ask Mike to do research on a variety of subjects of interest to him and us. Whether in a discipleship school format, leadership training, or missional development, if we would give out assignments or assign books to read, he would do it almost immediately. I noted his ability to research, resource, discover, mine-out information, and present it in well-written reporting format. Mike said to me while having coffee, earlier this year, that he felt he was to write a book. I asked him what subject and he told me *Fear*! I knew that he had battled with the subject of fear in its various forms for many years.

I told Mike, "I will support you in writing this book if you are willing to 'deal with your fears, first.'" Go first. Write as one who is on a journey to freedom, identify with the people you are writing to, and Father will use this as a testimonial tool to liberate people. True prophetic people who carry prophetic insight, grace, and anointing 'identify' with people they lead, write to, or minister. They do not rise above nor speak down to people, as ones who have 'it altogether;' rather, they come-along-side. They release the beautiful gift of mercy that they themselves have received and offer to others as *dispensers of the same*."

Mike has done this. My first reading of his first draft, my heart 'was pumped' for Mike. I don't know how many drafts were done, but the communication of his journey, interwoven with sound biblical truth, fully reflects what God has done for him and what He can do for all of us. That's encouraging. That's good news.

Since knowing Michael, he has always desired to love, serve, and encourage people forward. This time, he has done it in a new way. He invites his readers to embark upon a journey with him in being free from fear and all its relatives.

Pandemic has become the word for 2020. Most of us have never experienced a pandemic. However, since the Garden of Eden, fear has

Foreword

paralyzed humanity in pandemic proportions without respect of person or culture. The content in this book, "Conquering the Fear Pandemic," offers solid solutions in obtaining freedom from fear, and maintaining that freedom while setting others free.

Well done Michael. I trust that those who read will rejoice with Mike in his first written offering, while also joining with him in our own journey of freedom from the "fear virus" by embracing Father's love in its various forms. As servant leaders in his life, it's our honor to recommend this book to you.

Let me be clear, the Anointed One has set us free—not partially, but completely and wonderfully free! We must always cherish this truth and stubbornly refuse to go back into the bondage of our past. (Galatians 5:1, The Passion Translation)

Kenn & Cheryl Gill
Founders and Senior Apostolic Leaders
Ripple Effect Ministries of Calgary
Calgary, Alberta

1

A Gentle Whisper

One word from God can alter the trajectory of our lives forever. This word invites us into a journey with God that we may have never considered. My adventure began one hot July evening in 2015. A friend invited me to attend a meeting hosted by *Catch the Fire* ministries to hear a recognized prophetess, Isabel Allum, speak. He believed she had a word in season for my life, as at the time, I had been walking through a difficult season.

That night, Isabel gave me a seven-minute prophetic word that addressed my childhood and recent years with skilled precision. Her prophetic word to me mentioned there were books I needed to write. That word wrestled me because I struggled to express myself in writing due to being diagnosed with a learning disability. Even though I knew this word was accurate, I could not figure out how God would fulfill His Word.

Four years later, my American ministry friend, Dr. Don Hughes, invited me to join him on a ministry trip to a First Nations reservation for several days of ministry in Onion Lake, Saskatchewan, Canada. Onion Lake straddles the provincial border between Alberta and Saskatchewan about 30 miles north of the border town Lloydminster. The highway that leads into Onion Lake weaves back and forth across the provincial border.

This trip would be the second time I ministered with Don. Our mutual friend Gene Mansfield had connected Don to me. Gene had met me online in 2003 through a prophetic forum and built a trusted friendship. We met each other in person in the Summer of 2007 after Gene had married a woman from Onion Lake. Gene was visiting Calgary, Alberta, for a ministry trip. He had been invited to minister at a Full Gospel church and asked me to be part of his ministry team. It was one of the first times that someone had trusted me to minister publicly.

That trip solidified our friendship. Over the next few years, Gene introduced me to trusted ministers in his life. One of those ministers was Don.

One day, Gene invited me to talk with Don. During our conversation, Don discerned the prophetic call on my life and asked me to stay connected. In 2017, I was in the Tampa Bay, Florida area visiting a friend. Don happened to be 30 miles away. I contacted him, mentioning that I was in the region and inquired if we could connect in person. We met up and spent several hours swapping stories. At the end of our conversation,

Don mentioned an upcoming opportunity he had in Slave Lake, a small town about six hours north of Calgary, the following year and asked if I would be interested in ministering with him.

One year later, I joined Don on his Slave Lake trip. Our meetings were supercharged with the power of God and we saw powerful, lasting breakthroughs in many lives. Many people were healed and set free with the anointing that flowed. Others received timely, accurate words of life and encouragement. The success of the meetings in Slave Lake led Don to ask me to minister in Onion Lake with him.

The Onion Lake trip transpired four and a half years from the time I received the prophetic word from Isabel. While there, the Lord started to give me a word for 2020. A yearly word from God was not a new concept for me. I had done it previously. While waiting on the Lord, the Lord revealed the many times He opened the eyes of His people. The further I meditated; the Lord revealed the grip of fear that was influencing our world. I was aware of His supernatural presence hovering over my life and decided to fast and pray. One evening during that time, I had a dream. In this dream, a friend of mine was in a cave. There was a bonfire in the cave, and she was singing a popular worship song from the 1990s called "More Love, More Power[j]."

In the dream, I told her that she did not need more love and power, as she had the fullness of God living inside of her. Upon awakening the next morning, I did not give the dream much more thought.

A few days later, I casually mentioned the dream to someone I knew who interpreted dreams. Their response shocked me. "You and your friend are both living in caves of fear. You need to remove her from her cave. But first, you need to leave your cave." I felt perplexed. I did not believe that I was in any cave of fear. However, I knew in my heart I lived in fear of rejection.

I began to write some thoughts on fear that arose in my heart. When we live in fear, we rob ourselves of exploring the world beyond our bubbles, or experiences. Our preconceived ideas of freedom can trap us in a place of complacent behaviors, preventing us from realizing true liberty in our heart, while keeping us in a cave of self-protection. We might not realize the very thing we are asking God for may be standing and knocking on the door of our lives. God desires to bring us into His fulfillment of everything we have desired, and He has preordained, but it may not appear in the way we expect.

Fear may lead to fantasy and paranoia in our minds. It robs and blinds us, leading us to stay in the caves of life, and controls our environment. Fear only gives us the illusion of safety and leads into fantasy. Fantasy gives us an unrealistic view of life, masking itself as truth and freedom. Fear's fantasy cloaks itself in a perceived state that prevents us from confronting and facing the reality in which we all live. We need God's pure love to chase down these situations in our lives, in our minds, and in our hearts. It gently confronts the strongholds and ideas in our thinking, while calling us out from the false protection that has cloaked and blinded us.

This love will allow us to engage our world fully and authentically, and see the beauty and the brokenness that exists.

When we choose to break free from fear, we can receive the solutions and authentic hope to help the people around us who live in fear. After we leave our cave of fear, we realize there was nothing to fear. We must risk confronting the fear we lived in and embrace a healthy confidence in who we are. Only then, and with God's help, are we ready to receive a clear, unpolluted, healthy view of life, not given to fantasy and delusion. We then will be able to authentically walk in love with ourselves and people around us, as perfect, (complete and mature) love casts out and displaces all fear.

A few weeks after my cave revelation, I was sitting in my church service when my friend, Angela O'Connell, spoke about a new novel she read entitled: *The Girl Behind the Red Rope*,[ii] written by Christian author Ted Dekker. The book was a story about a young woman named Grace that lived in a faith community.

This faith community lived under a blanket of fear from an unseen enemy named the Fury. They were instructed by an angel to hide and wait until the Fury had purged Earth. They were forbidden to cross the red ropes that bordered their community. Once the Fury had purged the Earth, this community would then be safe to leave their region. I will not give away the details of the book, but it is an excellent read. Upon hearing her description of the book, I knew that I needed to read it.

I got the book for a Christmas gift and could not put it down. This book prodded away at my heart, inviting me to face my fear issues. It gently exposed my heart. At the same time, I began to see how easily fear ensnares our lives without us realizing. Often, we fail to see how fear influences our behaviors, thoughts, and actions.

At the same time, a revelation bubbled up in my spirit. I began to realize God was giving me a life message about overcoming fear. It was becoming an integral part of my mandate. However, I had to make a choice. In order for me to minister freedom to fears in others, I had to overcome the fears in my own life.

While I worked on the word that I received for 2020, the Lord highlighted to me that we are to operate in the Spirit of Might. We are not 'Chicken Little,' crying that the sky is falling. We are to rise in faith, declaring that the Kingdom of God is coming, and that we are not slaves to fear. We are to arise in our identity as His children, dearly loved and accepted by Him. Little did I know how prophetic these words were, as COVID-19 became part of the daily news a few weeks later.

I met with Kenn Gill to share with him the word the Lord was giving me for 2020. Kenn has been a pastor in my life for almost thirty years. He affirmed my prophetic word and asked if I would share it with our local church in Calgary. One caveat he had was for me to address my own personal fears first. That topic made me uncomfortable, as Kenn and I both knew that I struggled in that area. The word I was going to present to my church wrestled with my fears and insecurities. I realized how deeply my fear was entrenched. I did not want to deal with it. Deep down, I knew to be able to present the word authentically, I needed to face my fear.

With Kenn's words echoing in my spirit, I started exploring where fear began in my life. This journey led me to a discovery of how prevalent fear operates throughout the threads of our lives. I came to the realization; we all battle fear. However, we have the free will to overcome its crippling effects in our lives. Do we want an abundant joy-filled life, or do we want to live under a blanket of fear? It is our choice.

Let us invite Holy Spirit into the start of this journey. Jesus calls Holy Spirit the *paraclete*. In the Greek, *paraclete* means one who comes alongside like an advocate, or helper. Holy Spirt wants to guide and heal our lives. Pray with me now, "Holy Spirit, I welcome You at the beginning of this journey. Guide and comfort me as I choose to explore my fear and how it affected my life. I need the inner strength and courage from You to face and overcome my fear. Reveal to me how fear has affected me and bring me a fresh revelation of the healing You have for me."

2
Exploring the Labyrinth of Fear

What do I mean by a fear pandemic? Pandemics[iii] are wide-scale geographical events or diseases that affect an exceptionally high proportion of the population of a region, a nation, or the world. Our English word "pandemic" finds its origins from the Greek word *pandemos*. There are two Greek words that form *pandemos*. *Pan* meaning (all or every), *demos* meaning (the people). Fear, like a pandemic, impacts every person in some way or fashion, though the effects may differ. Both fear and pandemic events irreparably change the way we do life.

The New Testament writers used the Greek word *phobos* to describe fear. Our English word "phobia" originates from this word. In Greek mythology, Phobos was a Greek god who represented panic and flight. His twin brother was Deimos, the image of terror or dread.

The Hebrew language uses imagery to paint a picture or an emotion. Two words are used to describe fear: *Yirah* and *Pachad*.

Yirah is the sense a person feels when on holy or sacred ground. It invokes excitement or destiny, while stirring up emotions of respect, or a sense of awe or reverence. *Yirah* draws and invites us into the heart of God or the fear of the Lord.

Pachad is projected or imagined fear. It describes the emotions of panic, dread, terror, or disaster or the feeling of being startled by a sudden alarm. The word invokes an image of quaking and shaking from the guts.

What thoughts come to mind when you think about fear? Fear is a vast topic to tackle, and we can explore many facets. From the beginning of time, humans have battled it. Fear will continue to be part of our lives as long as we live. How we respond to fear is our choice.

People face fear in many ways. Some deny fear's existence in their lives, which is a form of inflated pride. Some battle fear daily in their minds and hearts, acknowledging it, but refuse to deal with it. Others recognize the influence fear has on their lives and choose to overcome it.

Before I delve into this topic, I want to make it clear that I am not authoring this book as a professional counselor or a registered psychologist. I do not claim to have any training in these areas. I want to offer keys gained from my life experience to assist you in your journey. My prayer is that you will discover victorious freedom over any fear that holds you captive.

Fear is a pandemic of epic proportions. There have been more casualties to fear than COVID-19, Ebola, the Spanish Flu, the Swine Flu, and the many other pandemics that have impacted our world. Fear's raging effects have affected every people group from every age since humans started to populate the Earth. Fear behaves much like a virus. Although we may not see the effects of it externally, fear is prevalent. If not treated, it can have deadly side effects. Not everyone who has the fear contagion physically dies, but many die internally to dreams, hopes, desires, and life itself.

Fear can blind us from living and enjoying ourselves, while it controls our every decision. It keeps those who can help us at arms-length. It can bring confusion into our minds and hearts, while influencing our decisions and relationships. It can cause paranoia and twist our realities, leading us into unrealistic fantasy lives. It can cause us to become so insecure that we live as social recluses erecting walls in our hearts, preventing us from entering healthy relationships. It can bring out a fighting attitude that causes collateral damage to relationships with our loved ones and friends, alike. It is a subtle force that will guide and manipulate our thinking at every turn.

Fear can also be a healthy emotion, protecting us from great danger. Think of a child touching a hot stove. Their reaction to the hot stove will reinforce a healthy boundary in their life. Ultimately, this helps to form their decision-making process.

No matter our background, each of us has been influenced by fear in some capacity throughout our life. If we trust God and open our hearts to Him, He will show us how fear has subtly influenced our lives. To become emotionally whole, we must deal with the way fear has shaped our lives. Once we choose to get emotionally healthy, we will be able to examine how fear has affected our decision-making and how God can help us make sound decisions. A spirit of fear will cripple our lives.

This diabolical spirit followed me everywhere I went, wreaking havoc on my life. It shackled itself to my emotions and my thinking patterns. It influenced me to the point where I lived in so much confusion that I could not make clear decisions for myself. Fear forced me to relinquish my emotions. Until I broke free of the grip of fear, I lived in deep chaos, self-doubt, and defeat. I struggled to build healthy relationships as fear's subtle lies would creep into my mind. It was the invisible robber, stealing the abundant life that God promised. It was the rudder that steered the direction of my life.

It is my prayer that as you read my stories and read this book, God will start to enlighten your heart and mind to see the positive and negative effects of fear in your life. May you find help as I did on my journey with trusted people that will speak to you and bring you into a victorious liberation of viewing yourself authentically as God sees you. May you emerge from the grips of fear into a supernatural dimension of the love of God. Let God's love flood your entire being, transforming you into a healthy, authentic individual, able to comprehend its depth, height, breadth, and length.

How does fear enter our hearts? In a time of personal reflection, I realized that I lived in fear my entire life. I also realized that God never intended that we live in fear, but there will be times of fear throughout life.

The psalmist writes, "What time I am afraid, I will have confidence in and put my trust and reliance in You." (Psalm 56:3, AMPC) It means that God will be with us in those times when we are afraid, and He will be there, walking alongside us. He will assist us in conquering fear's grip.

Later, in Psalm 139, the writer describes how we are knitted together fearfully and wonderfully; made in our mother's womb.

"For you created my inmost being; you knit me together in my mother's womb. I praise you because I am fearfully and wonderfully made; your works are wonderful, I know that full well." (Psalm 139:13-14, NIV)

This scripture leads me to the account where I believe fear entered my life. Scientists have discovered that babies in their mother's womb can feel, or pick up, the emotions of the external environment outside of the womb. A few weeks before my mother gave birth to me, she was working at a bank. A bank robber entered the branch and held a gun at her pregnant belly. At that moment, fear entered my being while in my mother's womb. I was targeted by fear before I was born.

From my earliest childhood memories, I recall battling fear. My mother recently shared a story with me when I was about three years old. I needed an operation on my belly button. When it came time for the procedure, my mother was instructed by a rude nurse to hand me over and walk away, and not look back. As she walked away from me, I started crying. I felt abandoned.

When I entered pre-school, I was hypersensitive to loud noises. The loud sound of the school bell would terrify me. I would cover my ears when I knew it was about to ring. I was also terrified of being around balloons. The sound of balloons popping frightened me immensely.

I also faced many years of teasing and bullying. The teasing made me fearful of my peers; I did not feel my childhood was typical. I lived in isolation and self-protection, all rooted in fear and rejection. Bullying only exacerbated my fears and affected my entire school experience, my learning abilities, and even led to struggles in the workforce. Fear led me down paths of rejection that would shape my life.

When we live in fear, we will do whatever it takes to protect ourselves from the rejection it brings, because fear and rejection partner together. They cause us to view life through cracked lenses, skewing our vision and outlook. We seek to control our environments, leading us to reject people that might have the ability to help us overcome fear. Fear makes us want to control our environment. We must displace that lie.

The older I got; the more fear entrenched itself within me. My parents wanted to protect me from people who sought to injure me. At times, they were sometimes blinded by those who genuinely wanted to help me. I struggled to differentiate from people who had pure agendas and those who did not. Even in my fear, I had a trusting disposition. When my parents saw what my peers were doing, they explained that not everyone was a friend. My struggle to make sense of everything going on, led to misunderstanding healthy boundaries. It was challenging to live a well-adjusted life.

My personality developed a social awkwardness, which influenced my external behaviors and habits. I became people-pleasing. At a personal cost, I would do whatever it took to get acceptance and love. But people-pleasing only magnified my feelings of low self-esteem and self-worth. I perceived my value as conditional, and the more I strove for approval, the less I received. My lack of boundaries caused victimization on more than one occasion in my life. Thankfully, some saw those taking advantage of me and started to protect and warn me of others' ulterior motives.

The root of people-pleasing is the fear of others, which causes us to seek affirmation and acceptance in a warped way. Proverbs states: "The fear of man brings a snare, but whoever leans on, trusts in, and puts his confidence in the Lord is safe and set on high." (Proverbs 29:25, AMPC) Fear of man will trap and cripple us. We may justify these behaviors thinking we are accepted and affirmed, but it only leads to frustration and futility. These behaviors can be exposed and displaced, as we invite God to transform our lives, while trusting Him to discern and disarm the fear.

When we live in fear, perfectionism and other suspect habits form our personalities. These act as coping mechanisms to protect ourselves. While we might be blind to them ourselves, others see how these coping mechanisms affect us and those around us. One thing we can do to help combat them is to allow trusted voices into our lives to help bring healing. If we allow the walls of our self-protection to fall, we can find healing from fear and its crippling effects.

Perfectionism is an entrenched lie that says our behavior and actions must be 100% perfect for our acceptance. If not dealt with, this can become a driving force into more anxiety and fear. We feel that if we do everything perfectly, we will finally gain acceptance and be free. It is merely an illusion. Often, perfectionism leads to more rejection and opens us up to rejecting others that God may have sent our way to bring help and betterment to our lives.

Even worse, there could be people that God sends our way, but we reject because they do not fit our preconceived ideas. We may justify these thoughts, yet wonder why we are lonely. When we believe the lies of perfectionism, we entrap ourselves in fear and sabotage ourselves in the process, leading to despair. In turn, we erroneously believe nothing we do is good enough, contributing to the false belief that no one is good enough. We fall into a pit of self-rejection and self-hatred. Depression takes root. To get healed, we need Holy Spirit to address the root system of perfectionism, which stems from an over-controlled, hyper, fear-filled environment. We want to work hard to be in control. Our drive for control stems from the chaotic traumas we faced when others domineered our lives in overprotective or other destructive ways.

In my school years, the more rejection and fear I faced, the greater I strove for perfection in my work. I believed if I did everything accurately and fault-free, I would finally find a safe place of acceptance. I watched my siblings and father succeed in school and business alike, and I still continuously struggled in futility and failure.

Early in my childhood, I was diagnosed with a learning disability that was exacerbated by a speech impediment. From this, a deep-rooted inferiority complex gripped me. I grappled with gaining confidence, as I did not believe I was good at anything.

I wrongly believed that I was not skilled, which made me unlovable. There were many instances I would come home from school feeling defeated and in tears because of the deep internal pain. The feeling of having no value to offer anyone and being unwanted resulted in deep self-deprecation. I lived under a cloud of fear, not knowing how I would survive the onslaught of bullying and abuse that I faced. The psychological warfare over my life weighed heavily on my parents and myself. The fear I lived under, coupled with social isolation, became unbearable. I could not comprehend what caused people to treat me with such contempt.

Fear has a way of twisting the truth of who we are and how we perceive our abilities that can result in crippling, deeply rooted low self-esteem and self-rejection. It causes us to lose confidence in our abilities and can self-sabotage healthy mindsets.

When graduating from high school, I attended my graduation ceremony with my parents, my grandfather, and a family friend. Having no grad date devastated me. I wanted to have a date like every other classmate. I felt like a lasting relationship with a woman was not in the cards for my life. After all, I believed, who wanted 'damaged goods'. My learning disability caused me stress that manifested as test anxiety, resulting in low marks on the provincial final exams. I lacked direction and internally, I believed that people saw me as 'damaged'.

The inferiority complex took hold of me and I found it difficult to proceed with post-secondary education. My fear of failure, social anxiety, and lack of confidence became a *perfect storm* in my life. This storm left me feeling directionless in life, and I had no idea where I fit in the world.

Fear reared its head again in the workplace. It became a massive adjustment. When I entered the workplace, I was oblivious to my social awkwardness. Both employers and employees misread my personality. I knew how to respect authority in the workplace, but because of my personality difficulties, I struggled with reading social cues. Those who did not want me around repeatedly made me out to be a threat. My fear and insecurity made me the target of bullies. I faced constant reprimands for poor performance. When bullied, I could never share my side of the story. I became repeatedly thrown to the curb like a used rag. These events led me to be dismissed on more than one occasion and re-enforced feelings of shame and failure.

I consistently struggled to understand why people were so mean to me. Not knowing who I was, or what I was doing incorrectly, intensified my rejection and pain. I just wanted to be like everyone else and enjoy relationships. 'Damaged goods' was the false message that seemed inscribed over my life. This lie contributed to false beliefs that I was meant to be an outcast my entire life.

I continually had feelings of failure and being a disappointment to my parents. Feelings of being unworthy of success and being able to enjoy the pleasures of life flooded my thought life daily.

I desperately wanted to have success in some form. I did not know how to discover it. When my younger siblings graduated high school, they were able to accomplish their life goals without the fear or struggle I had experienced. Everything I faced became an insurmountable struggle of failure.

I also struggled to connect and relate with my father. I perceived that he could not relate to my struggles. From my perspective, it appeared like everything my dad did was successful. When I was a teenager, my father stepped out on a new business venture. Everything worked out smoothly. He never showed issues of fear in his life. The culmination of events made me question why I felt like the black sheep of my family and why I faced consistent struggles.

Fear has a way of subconsciously damaging and influencing our behaviors. I was unaware of the damaging side effects that fear had caused to my personality. Looking back, I realize I made countless mistakes and miscues, and inadvertently crossed boundaries, but I was blinded. In church life, I struggled with forming relationships with peers in my age group. During this part of my journey, there was a group of older young adults who took an active interest in my life who became like older siblings. Their friendships helped kickstart my healing journey. If it had not been for these people, I may have shipwrecked my life.

The imprisonment of fear leaves a cloud of despair over our lives and a void of joy, hope, and love. Its psychological effects on my life left a limp that took years to dig out. When your entire life experience is fear, and you find freedom, you want to help others that are trapped by its deadly snare. Fear will so entrap a person that they want to capitulate to it. Do not give in. Fear only has power when we give in to its grip.

Exploring the Labyrinth of Fear

Later, I will provide tools I used to overcome fear in my healing journey. The miracle in my life was that I never gave up, even though there were many times that it looked so bleak.

Out of everything I faced, I can give you authentic hope. Fear does not need to control your life. Jesus came to give us abundant life. The more I healed from my fear, the more hope I received that I could give to others.

Let me give you a story of how I started to heal from the trauma I faced. Earlier in this chapter, I mentioned my fear of loud noises and how a gun was held to my mother's womb. Around 2007, God brought a trusted young man into my life and he had an interest in firearms. I had never touched guns and was extremely nervous around them. He realized my nervousness and decided to take me to a gun range to aid me in overcoming this fear. That day became a life-defining moment!

That afternoon, my friend and I drove to a rural Alberta outdoor gun range. It was only the two of us at the range and he started to instruct me how to properly handle a gun. Confidence rose within me as I took my first shots with a .22 rifle. The more rounds I shot; a fresh, new thrill of freedom filled my being. While we were shooting targets, a murder of crows flew over the gun range. My friend encouraged me to target the birds. I did not think I would be able to hit the birds but at his insistence, I took several shots. Suddenly, my friend looked at me astonished. He told me that I had successfully shot a crow out of the air and it was a difficult accomplishment. We were both thrilled. That day changed my life. I decided to get my gun license, and that experience built fresh confidence within me to conquer fear in other areas of my life.

Right now, begin reflecting on your life. Can you perceive the hand of a loving God? If not, invite Him to reveal His workings in your life, both in your good moments and trying moments. Have others come into your life to offer hope and encouragement to you when needed? Reflect on what benefit they brought you in your journey, and how their actions may have empowered you. Also, examine your behavior and thought processes. Can you identify any areas that might have caused people to misinterpret you? Welcome God to begin gently mending the damaged areas of your life and minister His love to your heart.

3

COVID-19

During February of 2020, the news media announced a new respiratory virus infecting people had originated from China. Reports started to emerge and spread through the media how people were becoming extremely sick or even dying from this new virus.

Initially, it started as obscure stories. At the end of January, the United States President, Donald Trump, took decisive action against China by closing the United States to travel from China. Trump faced many comments calling him and his actions xenophobic and racist from politicians and the left-leaning media. Throughout February, cases in China started to increase and the voice of fear of this illness echoed throughout the media. The virus and fear started to spread world-wide, culminating in the World Health Organization declaring a world pandemic on March 11th.

Conquering the Fear Pandemic

The world rocked with the announcement. The international community went into full-blown panic and fear. Our world was transformed overnight. It was as if a bomb was dropped in our world and everyone felt the sudden hysteria. I awoke one morning the week of March 11th seeing the headlines on a news alert that the stock market was due to open 1000 points lower. I knew then and there; fear was going to be the "new norm" and that we were in for a rough road. As the pandemic unfolded, words like *social distancing* and *flattening the curve* became entrenched in the pop culture. The left leaning media and the Democratic party blamed President Trump for not reacting fast enough. People became paranoid about their neighbors and friends. It seemed like overnight, people who were once close to each other, became very distant and cold. People began to snitch on their neighbors for coming too close to them. Suspicion became pervasive in the minds of many. Everyone was perceived as a potential carrier of this virus, and people who lived in fear of each other became a 'new normal'.

Every day, the news media would paint COVID-19 in the bleakest of scenarios, proclaiming boldly that millions could be infected and die from the pandemic. From my observation, it became very apparent how far the media would take their narratives and spin the fear. Broadcasts would show the number of cases and deaths on graphs and the media voices would proclaim, "Stay at home. Limit the spread." Fear became the new narrative of the day, much like the events of September 11, 2001, when planes crashed into the World Trade Centre in New York and other places killing 2977 people[iv]. These events forever changed the United States foreign policy of handling security at airports and other points of entry. Likewise, this pandemic has similarly changed the world. People took the message seriously. The voice of fear seemed to reverberate into every corner of society.

In the face of this new fear, companies started to massively lay off staff and those who would survive being laid off would start to work from home. Churches pivoted to online services. Malls and businesses alike shut their doors to the public or implemented extremely strict guidelines if they remained open. Restaurants also closed their doors to the public and events and sporting events were canceled. The Canadian/USA land border was shut to travel, except essential business travel. In Canada, the Canadian government processed over one million applications for unemployment insurance by the end of March 2020. That number grew to well over three million claims by the end of April 2020. Before COVID-19, the United States had been enjoying a booming economy under President Trump. Suddenly, millions were unemployed. The coronavirus trumped every topic and seemed to be on the lips of everyone. It appeared that overnight, the fear of COVID-19 spread like wildfire. People were locked down in fear of this unknown enemy.

Throughout this time, I kept hearing the voice of God speaking peace to my heart. I decided that the voice of fear was not going to control me through it all. As coworkers, friends, and family listened to the media daily, I distinctly remember hearing the Lord speak, "My people are listening to the wrong voice. The voice of fear controls their actions and behavior. My sheep need to hear My voice and the voice of a stranger, they will not follow."

I believe the Lord showed me that people relied on the voice of the media more than they relied on God's Word. I could hear it in friends and family alike. We made the voice of fear stronger than the voice of our Good Shepherd.

We all have a choice. We can choose to follow the voice of fear or follow the voice of faith that speaks peace. The COVID-19 crisis created an opportune time that has presented itself to us. In every crisis, there is an opportunity. We need to discover the opportunity that is being presented during crisis and then capitalize on it. Our heart is revealed during moments of crisis. God's Spirit searches our hearts, revealing the foundations of our lives. The more we allow fear to rule our hearts, the harder it is to hear the voice of the Lord in our lives, and the darker our path becomes. The more we prioritize the voice of faith, the more opportunities we will see in our lives, and the more we will see the glory of God. It is time that we allow the love of God to dispel the voice of fear and arise as modern-day givers of hope to the world around us.

If we allow God's perfect love to dwell in our hearts, the love of God will extinguish the fear that pervades our lives. The more we open ourselves to the love of God in our hearts, the less control we want in our lives. Love brings freedom to embrace people freely without agendas and fear. Love brings comfort and security to those around us. Love dispels rejection, fear, and control. Authentic love brings hope and joy to people and the more we choose to walk in love, the easier life is for us. Love will be tested, and true love is not easy, but it is far greater than living in fear.

It has become very apparent out of the COVID-19 pandemic how powerful the force of fear can become and how easily it can consume us if left unchecked. COVID-19 became more of a fear pandemic, rather than a medical issue due to the fallout that it created. Yes, there have been people infected with a virus. Our lives have all been affected because of this virus, but the true pandemic is the power we give fear to rule our hearts. To the degree we allow fear to control us, reveals the depth we do not trust God. We have given the voice of our media control and to sway our opinions about others. The media has shaped how we perceive reality, more than we have allowed the voice of our Good Shepherd to lead us. We all hear voices; it is up to us to decide what voice we follow. The media was full of worst-case scenarios, leading us to panic more than necessary. If we had just followed common sense, we would not have been so caught up in fear. Fear tends to sensationalize while influencing and manipulating our thinking, leading us to fall into extreme, irrational thinking.

4

The Power of Words

When I started assembling my thoughts on fear, I felt led to explore the power of our words and how they contribute to the development of fear in our lives. There is a direct correlation between fear and the power of words. It took me back to the scripture where Jesus said, "The words I have spoken to you are spirit and are life." (John 6:63, ESV) The word for "spirit" in the Greek is the word *pneuma*. *Pneuma* defined is the disposition or influence which fills and governs the soul of anyone. It can also refer to a blast, a wind, a breath, or an inspiration.

When Jesus said His words are spirit and life, He knew words carry influence. They can fill a person's innermost being and influence their thoughts and actions. This can cause a person to fall into fear, or to rise in faith in powerful ways. I was taken back to my childhood and the many words people labeled me. Words like slow, loser, unable to learn, stupid, or dumb negatively affected me. It also took me back to a situation several years ago where I faced a legal matter with an individual who had chosen to defraud me financially.

I had won a legal judgment in civil court against someone who had taken a significant sum of money from me, and I was trying to collect on the judgment. This person sent repeated e-mails claiming he had sent the money to me. I relentlessly tried to collect what was legally mine, but the tone of his emails became increasingly more threatening. Daily, I received emails from him and the tone of them scared me. I began envisioning this man showing up on my doorstep seeking to harm me. His words and actions led me to fall into a pit of fear. The tone the person was using had *pneuma* behind it, and it was not life-giving in any way. It was twisted and dark, sowing confusion and fear in my heart. A nauseous feeling would overwhelm me every time I received another email. I finally had to change my personal email. I also faced numerous stalking messages and posts on my social media account, such that I had to restrict my settings. I had to go to the police several times to get this man to stop contacting me and interfering with my life. Eventually, I got a satisfactory resolution from the police.

When I reflect on this situation, I realize how much power our words have on others. It makes me aware of how we can either become imprisoned by fear from others' words or how we can rise in faith. The tone and words this man projected through his emails reflected a contamination of fear and hatred that he carried internally towards people.

The Power of Words

In the Greek language, there are two words that translate "word". One is *logos* which refers to the Written Word and the second word is *rhema*. *Rhema* is the quickened Word of God into our spirits. When God speaks to us through the scriptures, or into our spirit through a personal word, the effect is a *rhema* Word; a quickening or a jumping in our spirit. It could be a word of caution, an affirmation, a correction, or a promise of God over our lives. The quickening *rhema* empowers our entire being. Words on a page do not have power, it is the *pneuma* behind the *rhema* that has the power. God's Spirit quickens our whole being and activates our faith. Likewise, the enemy's words will try to cause us to fall into fear, and influence our entire being. In my case, the *pneuma* behind the man who defrauded me was attempting to get me to capitulate to a spirit of fear. However, the very power of the *pneuma* of God that gives life to our being was at work to calm my fears and to bring me into a new measure of faith.

I faced another situation in life where God brought me into a new dimension of faith through the power of His quickened Word. This time, the *rhema* word spoke to my fear and brought me into a whole new understanding of who God is. This event did not deny the influence of the fear; however, it spoke right to the spirit of fear and brought me into a supernatural dimension of faith.

In August of 2003, I was visiting South Wales. At the end of the trip, I wanted to get a memoir from my travels. The person I was staying with took me to a mall where we were looking at some elegant Swiss watches. I ended up finding a beautiful watch that I had seen and liked in Canada.

The watch retailed for over $2000 in Canada. There it was sitting before me, brand new in the box for about £330, or about $700 CAD at a reputable dealer, complete with warranty. The only problem was I did not have the money to buy it.

The person I was with saw the watch catch my interest. He was a successful businessman and property investor. He knew my situation. I had no money to buy this timepiece, but I decided to try it on. The watch fit perfectly. I loved how it felt on me, and I wanted to purchase it. I knew it looked good. However, I realized there was no possibility of buying it, because I could not justify putting $700 on my credit card. I believed it would be financially irresponsible.

The gentleman asked me what my thoughts were on the watch. He could tell I was extremely interested in it. I told him how much I liked the timepiece and thought it suited me, but I could see no possibility of it being a reality at the time. I shared with him how I barely had enough money in my bank account and that there was no way I could afford something this expensive. Furthermore, I refused to cripple myself in debt on something like a watch. It was a luxury I simply could not justify. He then posed a question. He asked me what my spirit was telling me, not my head. I had to silence my anxious thoughts swirling around in my head. The negative bombardment said to me that there was no way I could justify something that extravagant and the nagging feeling of what people would think if I would buy it. Yet deep down within the depths of my heart, I heard the still small voice of the Lord whisper peacefully, "Buy the watch, son."

I wanted to so rebuke the idea that invaded my thoughts. It was not what I wanted to hear. It rudely interrupted my fearful thoughts and brought me a calming peace. I felt shaken to my core and rebuked the thought. Noticing that I was visibly distracted, the gentleman I was with asked me what was bothering me. I explained how I believed God was encouraging me to step out in faith to buy the extravagant watch. Yet I knew, there was no way I could afford it. This businessman then told me how he faced a similar situation when he bought his first property and was extremely nervous, except he knew that God had spoken to him. We discussed the pros and cons of it, and it alleviated some of the fear, but the fearful voice in my head kept pounding back, "You don't have the money. You will get in trouble with your credit card company. Your parents will think you are crazy." These thoughts were like a rapid-firing machine gun. I finally had to pull back again and ask for a confirmation from the Lord. Once More, the cool breeze of the voice of God calmed the fears inside my heart. It was the strangest sensation to have the voice of fear and the voice of the Spirit of Life speak at the same time.

For about thirty minutes, I wrestled back and forth; I finally decided to buy the watch, regardless of the consequences. We walked back to the store. The store clerk proceeded to fill out the warranty card and asked for my credit card. Slowly, I handed over my credit card, shaking internally like a leaf. It was one of the longest moments of my life. I remember the nervous feeling, half expecting that this wealthy person I was with, at any moment, was going to hand his card over to buy it for me, instead. That never transpired. I signed my receipt and several seconds later, I was the owner of this new Swiss watch. Inside of me, there was an internal joy, yet a nervousness that I could not shake. I had stepped out in faith on something so big. The businessman told me how proud he was of me and we walked out of the store. There was a side of me still wondering if I was foolish or in presumption, or if I had truly heard the voice of God.

I wore that watch home from my trip, and I realized I still had to pay for it. I did not know how that would be a reality, as I did not have a job waiting for me back in Canada. I knew I did not have the resources and without options, I was feeling apprehensive. Shortly after coming home, I was out for an evening and I ran into an old friend. She and the friend she was with saw the new watch on me and asked me about it. I shared the story with them about the watch and they were very moved by the story of stepping out in faith. The next day, she called me telling me they wanted to drop by and visit. I invited them in, and her friend told me how much my faith had inspired his walk and handed me the exact amount I needed to pay off the watch. I was blown away. God had provided the monies needed to pay off my watch. It felt like a kiss from Heaven that God knew I was supposed to have it and He provided according to His riches, not mine. Whenever I wore that watch, it reminded me of God's provision over my life and that I was not to live in fear, but the realm of supernatural faith that dispels fear.

The Power of Words

The voice of fear first entered humanity when Adam and Eve were in the Garden. The serpent came to Eve ready to assault God's goodness towards us. The serpent came to twist the goodness of God saying, "Did God really say?" The twisting of the word allowed fear to enter the heart of Eve. Instead of rising in her spiritual authority, Eve gave her authority away. When she and Adam ate of the fruit from the tree of the knowledge of good and evil, they realized their nakedness, lived afraid of God, and hid from Him in the Garden. Their relationship with God changed from this one action. Since the beginning of Creation, humans were meant to have fellowship with God. Now, that relationship was severed.

The power of words can twist thoughts and make one believe almost any narrative you want them to believe about a situation, a person, or a people group. The words on the page are not the issue. It is the *pneuma* behind the words that can influence how a person views the situation a writer is communicating. The writer, just like the people reading the words, is influenced by all sorts of sources when they write or speak. When we speak, we are simply using the air to form the words. We use our hands to write. However, there is a greater force behind the words. Often, we do not realize what we are being influenced by unless we take a moment to self-reflect. Could our motivation be fear or a personal bias towards people? Are we secretly desiring people to take our viewpoint? Could we be manipulated by controlling forces? These are interesting thoughts to examine.

Conquering the Fear Pandemic

During my personal study of world history, I discovered something startling, while examining the history of Adolf Hitler's *Third Reich*[v]. In Nazi Germany, the way the press described the Jewish people led to an entire people group being persecuted and viewed as "ones to be feared". Adolf Hitler realized the power behind his words could sway public opinion and cause a fear pandemic towards different people groups. Hitler utilized the media through Joseph Goebbels to influence the German people to repudiate the Jews that were living in Germany. The manipulative tactics were effective. Germans developed a hatred for Jews, targeting them ruthlessly with threats and murderous actions. When World War II ended with Germany in shambles, the veil of fear lifted the blinders off the German people. They were in shock when realizing what they had believed for nearly fifteen years. Some could never accept the reality of what was being exposed and denied it. Others were in total shock of the reality that Hitler had painted for them and wanted to make amends.

As Jesus followers, we are called to be the light of the world and sons and daughters of God. That is our true identity. If we are to reflect the light of the world, we must choose to push passed our fears and reflect the light of God's goodness to the world around us. I believe that the more we shine with God's presence, the more authentic and real we will become. The more we heal from the grip of fear in our hearts, the more we will be able to accurately reflect the heart of God to many. Paul told the Galatian church that it was for freedom that Christ has set us free and we were no longer to be subject to a yoke of bondage. This picture Paul paints is one of a comparison between fear and faith. He contrasts life in

The Power of Words

Christ to life under fear, while pointing to our true birthright and inheritance.

Even as COVID-19 spread like wildfire across the globe, governments used their power to use words to influence people. Think back at the times you saw or read signs that exhorted you to stay inside, *limit the spread*, *practice social distancing*, and *keep six feet apart from each other*. These words and the way they were written caused people to live in fear of the virus and each other. It became an all-pervasive tool to spread fear, and we entertained the *pneuma* behind the words. The words on these signs were designed to align our behavior with a desired action. This was used by governments, businesses, and interest groups alike to align the thoughts and actions of people with what they wanted. And it worked. People listened to the media and relinquished their free wills.

Invite Holy Spirit right now to break any word curses that have been spoken, declared, or imposed over your life. These word curses may have controlled your thoughts or allowed fear into your life. Let Him reveal the words that have been spoken over you that crippled your life. Ask God to forgive you for taking any of them on as part of your identity and choose to forgive those who have sinned against you by what they have said. You are not what has been spoken over you. You are what your Heavenly Father says about you. Before Jesus started His ministry, the Father spoke His affirmation over Him, and the Father does the same for you. You are His beloved son or daughter in whom He is well pleased.

The power of God's Word will bring you into great security. Will you allow Him today to do that for you?

5

Shame's Crippling Effects

Shame can be a vicious device that causes people to fall into fear's grip. Before the fall, Adam and Eve were never aware of their nakedness and they had no shame. They lived in freedom and fellowship with God and with each other. They were able to enjoy an authentic, true relationship without any concern. They were able to walk with God in the cool of the day and enjoy a healthy relationship with one another.

Shame entered humanity after Adam and Eve disobeyed God by eating from the tree of the knowledge of good and evil in the Garden of Eden. Shame became a major tool used by satan to bring fear into people across the Earth.

People have described shame as a painful feeling in oneself about their identity. It doesn't necessarily depend on having done anything wrong. It has more to do with how a person feels about themselves and how they appear to others. People who live under shame consistently feel bad about themselves. If not dealt with, shame can severely paralyze a person's life by fanning into flame thoughts that they are no good.

Shame is a powerful companion of fear. If we shame ourselves or others shame us, it becomes a driving force to live in fear of others. If unchecked, this can lead to low personal self-worth. It causes us to strive for the approval of others. Fear and shame work hand in glove to cripple our thought life. The more one is shamed, the more one falls into fear.

The psychological effects of shame coming through childhood wounding can devastate someone's emotional well-being into their adult years. The more a person is shamed, the harder it is to rise above it. Moreover, the more shame that a person faces, the more they will live in fear of themselves, their abilities, and their relationships. Confidence erodes in their lives. Unless shame is overcome, it results in a crippling blow to a person's outlook on life. Fear and shame will overwhelm a person, such that it will manifest a lack of healthy, Godly self-love, a lack of confidence, and depressive states. Feelings of despair and hopelessness rob a person from believing and enjoying God's goodness.

Shame can lead a person into suicidal tendencies. A shame-filled person is often fear-filled and will do anything to save face or protect themselves. Undealt with, shame can also lead a person into addictive behaviors to try to mask the internalized shame.

Shame's Crippling Effects

At the root of shame is an underlying inferiority complex that says, "I am flawed, I must be bad! I am not worth anything." Shame leads a person into a self-destructive lifestyle. Those who are bullied usually have huge shame issues and fear issues, and are typically very lonely. Unless unhealed shame is dealt with, a person will live a life full of self-sabotage, and not achieve their true purpose, never arising to their full potential.

How is shame visible in a parent's life? As a parent, do you ever think or feel ashamed because of what has happened to your children in life? Perhaps your child struggled in school and your friend's children are top performers. You may feel deep shame about your own children's lack of success. You may compare their lack of success to another's. You can inadvertently bring shame onto your children, because you do not want to lose face with your friends. You want to look good in your friend's eyes and if your children do not meet your expectations, you can bring fear and shame upon them because of your feelings.

From my observation, there are certain cultures on Earth in which the parents put inadvertent shame upon their children. In the parent's eyes, the child has not lived up to the norms that their culture expects of them. If the child did not live up to the ideals or the expectations of the home, they tend to face shame more often, because the parental construct wants to save face in view of friends. Kenn Gill, my pastor, has often mentioned that everyone must surrender their culture of origin to the cross of Christ, while establishing and embracing a Biblical worldview into the home to combat the shame.

Have you ever dealt with someone who is narcissistic? Narcissistic individuals have massive undealt shame issues. They love to project their negative self-worth onto others' lives. Often, they have so much shame in their own life, that they "blame shift" it onto others to prevent them from having to deal with their low self-confidence and low self-worth. Narcissism becomes an inflated arrogance in a person's personality at the expense of others. They have fragile self-worth and love to lash out at others when they feel threatened.

Narcissistic behavior projects shame on others. Narcissist individuals enjoy making others feel bad and enjoy watching how their sinister behavior has affected their victims. They honestly think they are right and everyone else is wrong. By shaming another person, the narcissist inflates their ego. They love to rage against those they have exploited, as they have never been able to deal with their own behavior. Internally, they hate the negative shaming they have endured and love to cover it up by placing it onto others and making others feel ashamed.

Social shaming has become a new phenomenon that has arisen in these days. People use social shaming to bring others into fear and subjection to their will. Social shaming involves public humiliation on a person or people group for their behaviors and/or actions; to conform and control their behaviors to fit a social norm. It can be done in person or it can be done over the internet. It is a form of 'mob justice,' a form of bullying. In recent years, we focused on standing up for those who have faced bullying and focused on bullying's negative effects. Now, all of sudden, it is socially acceptable to bully and shame people for their beliefs when they differ from a herd mentality or a special interest group.

These days, people love to call others out without mercy. It has weaponized people in many ways, with the voice of control or manipulation. Social shaming can target anyone, at any time, and is most used on social media. Social media has become a tool and a weapon to influence people's views on various social topics. Social media has given a voice to people to gang up and bully others into fear and can be very destructive to those it reaches. Never in our history have people had such an effective way of changing people's perspectives or destroying people's lives like today. We must be cognizant of the dangerous negative effects of social shaming, as there have been many people whose lives have been permanently damaged or destroyed due to social shaming.

Social shaming loves to empower insecurity in others, creating a gang-like mentality. People think they are doing a favor to others by social shaming. They want to make the so-called "offending party," a scapegoat. Social shaming puts pressure on offending parties to reconsider, or change their stance on an issue. They desire to have the target individual capitulate their stance, or conform their behaviors, to the will of others.

Several years back, I befriended a married couple. Over the years of friendship, my battle with shame and wounded personality seemed to irritate the husband. It seemed no matter what I did or said or believed, he always tried to force his beliefs onto me. One Christmas, they were coming for a visit to my home city for a few weeks. In my quiet time, the Lord gently whispered to me, "Be careful how much time you spend with this couple. If you don't, you will have to choose between following Me and your friendship with them." Little did I realize how that warning would play out.

The first few days of their visit seemed to go normally. However, the more time I spent with them; the shaming escalated. One night, we were eating dinner at a mutual friend's house. At the table, the topic came up about my beliefs. Right then, they began shaming me in front of everyone. I left feeling very embarrassed. The last day of their trip finally arrived and I was fed up. The day started normally, but it seemed they were determined to change my thinking. Point blank, they asked, "Where do we stand to speak into your life about anything?" I told them flat out that they had no permission to speak into my life about anything, as I was tired of the non-stop nitpicking and bullying. With that, they dropped me off at a bus station and I was left to find my way home. They were infuriated by my response and drove off. It was the last time I would ever see them or talk with them.

On my way home, I cried out to the Lord to ask Him what happened. He gently whispered to my spirit, "I told you that you had to choose between your call that I gave you and your relationship with your friends if you weren't careful." I realized then and there I could not maintain a relationship with the couple for a long time, if ever. We were on two separate journeys and I did not need to walk theirs. A few years later, they tried to come back into my life, and I had to erect boundaries. When I put up my boundaries, they tried to shame me for having them in place. Their reply demonstrated to me that I had made the right choice. The dynamics were still unhealthy.

Shame is not the same thing as guilt. We have already defined "shame" as feeling badly about one's self. "Guilt" is feeling badly about an action we have taken. It is important to differentiate the two as some people see shame and guilt as the same. They are not. Both can lead to fear but in separate ways. When we live in guilt, we may fear the repercussions of our actions. We need to own up to how our actions have affected others. When Judas betrayed Jesus for thirty pieces of silver, he was overcome with guilt for knowing that Jesus was innocent. It was the one/two combination of guilt and shame that drove this chosen disciple to take his life.

Shame can be a form of pride in our life. We can get so comfortable in hiding in our shame that we use it as a form of control. We do not want others to see our weaknesses and flaws. But the truth of the matter is that humility neutralizes our pride and our shame. Humility recognizes our need for healing from shame. Humility is the acknowledgment of God's grace in our weak condition and the awareness that we are dependent upon His finished work and His righteousness.

Shame will also keep us from living in the fullness of God's provision and promotion. A person who wrestles with shame will never seek after promotions, jobs, or relationships, as they do not feel worthy or deserving of them. Until recently in my life, I always tried to play it safe and never pursued relationships with young women. I hid from it as I never saw myself as worthy of love or acceptance. I cloaked it in hyper-spirituality saying that I was waiting on God. Others had belittled my personality many times. "What kind of woman would want you?" they would say in jest. Out of that ungodly belief, I lived in my introverted world, not seeking to open myself up to hurt.

I faced the same struggle at work from others when they would say things like, "You aren't worthy of that promotion or that job as you have to put in your time at the bottom." Or, "You can't go after that job. Why would they hire you? You don't have what it takes." These messages reinforced my internal shame. I felt that people saw me as a second-rate individual and deserved to be at the bottom of the barrel all my life. I felt like I was undeserving of good things in life and always meant to be everyone's servant my entire life. This manifested in a massive fear of failure, leading me to avoid taking chances or risks. I was imprisoned in my shame, paralyzed by fear, and had no idea how to get unstuck.

On my own, I never would have been able to admit that I had shame in my heart. But my pastor, Kenn Gill, saw what was going on in my inner world. We would have coffee meetings and he would tell me gently many times, "I can help you if you'll let me, Mike. You have some things that are holding you back. Would you consider seeing a counselor?" I knew he was right, yet because of the constant internal pressure to conform to others, I avoided the topic.

Shame's Crippling Effects

I finally realized that unless I dealt with my shame, I would remain crippled for the rest of my life. I summoned the courage to go meet with a professional counselor named Graham Bretherick who helped me peel back the shackles of fear, shame, and a host of other issues. Thanks to Graham's help, and Kenn's support and love, I was able to make a lot of progress in seeing who I really was. This process kickstarted my emotional healing journey.

Just a sidenote, if you want some excellent material on anger, shame, or fear, I highly recommend Graham's books. He has authored three excellent books that are easy to read and can help people begin their healing journey. *Healing Life's Hurts*[vi] deals with anger and working through anger issues. *Free to be Me*[vii] is his book on shame and *The Fear Shift*[viii] is his book on fear. All three are available through Amazon or *Run Free Ministries* at www.runfreecouselling.com. They are excellent resources to assist anyone who wants to overcome the issues of the heart from a Biblical perspective.

There is an account in the book of 2 Samuel about a grandson of King Saul who struggled with shame named Mephibosheth. Mephibosheth was dropped by his nurse when he was young, leaving him crippled for life. The Hebrew name *Mephibosheth* means "from the mouth of shame." He spent his entire life feeling like he was the enemy of Israel; unworthy, loathing, and fearing his life. Mephibosheth was from a place called *Lo-Debar*. *Lo-Debar* translated from the Hebrew means "no pasture, communication, or word." It was a non-descript town and considered a ghetto.

The next king of Israel, David, wanted to show kindness to the house of Saul for the sake of the covenant that David had made with Saul's son Jonathan. When he heard that Saul's grandson was still alive, David called for Mephibosheth. Mephibosheth feared for his life, as it was the tradition of the day that if a king were killed or conquered, all his descendants would be killed by the next king. Naturally, Mephibosheth felt that he would be taken out. David, however, moved by the kindness of God, wanted to give Mephibosheth a seat of honor at the king's table. Initially, Mephibosheth was not able to receive the honor. He felt he was nothing more than a dead dog and a cripple. David persisted, and Mephibosheth finally relented. It was Mephibosheth who did not know about the covenant that David had made with Jonathan. Mephibosheth got the surprise of his life when David told him that he was going to be honored and seated at the king's table for the rest of his life, just like one of the king's sons. It was David who brought dignity and healing to Mephibosheth's life. Interestingly, after this account, the scriptures never recall that Mephibosheth called himself as a cripple or a dead dog. Could it be that David's kindness towards Mephibosheth brought healing to Mephibosheth's heart of shame?

When I came out of high school, I was not accustomed to people wanting to be my friend. However, that was about to change. My church had started a young adult ministry. It was at this time, that I met two brothers and their family who were several years older than me. Both brothers became good friends and accepted me into their family like a younger brother.

Shame's Crippling Effects

I was invited into their family home and hearts and given unconditional acceptance. They worked in a family-run automotive shop that their mother and father had started years prior. I found myself spending hours at their autobody shop and the family home on countless occasions. Their mom, 'Gramma' as she would be lovingly called by her sons, would always open her heart and home to me, always making sure I had food and would encourage me of God's goodness. She and her sons were pillars in my life while I struggled to find my way in the world. They never shamed me in my struggles and stood beside me and encouraged me through my struggles.

Through my quarter-century relationship with this family, I have shared many joyful moments and many tears, as well. This family found a way of encouraging my faith, while going out of their way to help me when they could. It was through the love that this family showed me, little by little, that helped me heal my fear and my shame. We always have had fun connecting on our love of cars and faith alike. I am truly thankful for these friends who have been there through the thick and thin and who never judged me for my unique life journey.

It is in the heart of God to see our lives completely healed of ungodly shame and fear. We were never meant to live shame and fear-filled lives, but to live in total freedom from shame and fear. The finished work of Jesus on the Cross paid for our shame. Unhealed shame robs us of living the abundant life that Jesus promised us. As we heal from the shame and fear that cripples us, we can rise in a fresh, confident outlook on our lives.

We can believe, hope, and dream again. We do not have to be a slave to shame and fear in our lives. One of the best tools that I have found working through deep shame issues has been seeing a counselor. Holy Spirit filled counselors are skilled at helping us see where we have believed lies about ourselves and to see the lies that have ensnared us. They can lovingly confront the issues that are at the core of our being, bringing understanding and revelation to areas that need healing.

The more we are healed, the more authentic love can flow out of us, and the more we will see life clearly. Pure love can help disarm and displace the shame that we carry. It is the amazing grace of God that can flow into the wounds of our shame and that can bring healing to our fears. We cannot remove shame in and of ourselves. We need Jesus to be the one who ministers to our hearts and brings healing to us. It is His finished work at the Cross that displaces the shame in our hearts. Jesus used the word *tetelestai* at the Cross to describe the finished work He accomplished. *Tetelestai* is a Greek work used to describe when a certificate of a debt, or taxes, had been paid for in full. Archeologists have found receipts with this wording on certificates in their digs from the days of the Roman Empire.

When Jesus died on the Cross for our shame, He scorned the shame of what the Cross represented. He was crucified in shame, but conquered all shame. Those who were crucified were openly naked for the world to see. It was to reinforce to those who were being crucified that it was the most shameful form of death. It usually took days for the accused to die by crucifixion. The body would rot and would remain upon the crossbeam for days. Those crucified by the Roman government would be used as an example to anyone who stood up to the government of Rome. Originally, crucifixion was reserved for slaves and criminals; only in extreme cases would Roman citizens face crucifixion.

Shame had no power over Jesus, and shame will have no power over us if we allow the Lord to heal our hearts. We can be free as God intended us to be, authentically loved and accepted. Jesus scorned the shame of the Cross. He was crucified in weakness, but rose in victory. It was a total victory over shame. That victory can be yours today.

Why not welcome Holy Spirit to minister to the shame in your heart? In addition, a trained Holy Spirit-filled counselor or psychologist can be used to untangle you from behaviors in your life that may have integrated into your personality. Jesus scorned shame at the Cross. Pray into this and let Holy Spirit work in your heart right now, "Holy Spirit, I recognize that shame has no place in my life. Jesus took my shame at the Cross and I choose to let it go. I receive the acceptance that Jesus gave me. I ask You to silence every condemning thought and voice of shame in my life. I choose to believe the promises of God over my life. I choose Your acceptance and love for me, which is not rooted in performance nor conditional. I choose to receive Your unconditional acceptance. Holy Spirit, go to the depth of the shame I have felt and root it out of me. Dispel the darkness of my shame and allow me to grab onto Your eternal hope. You are the glory and the lifter of my head and I choose, by an act of my will, to walk shame-free and guilt-free. Amen."

6

Abuse & Bullying

Earlier, I described my childhood and some of the abuse and bullying I faced. This influenced my personality and my behavior. Abuse continued throughout my teenage years. By twelve years of age, I was physically smaller and weaker than my peers. I was not athletic and had poor coordination. When young men enter their teens, they tend to compare themselves to others. They may exercise their physical dominance over weaker peers to reinforce a sense of security in themselves.

My physical limitations adversely affected my life.

How did this play out? My sensitive personality and fearful disposition worsened as I got older. I can recall many times my change clothes for gym class were thrown into the urinals of the boy's change room. At the same time, I faced the roughhousing of the boys trying to exercise their masculine dominance. Since I was the smallest and weakest, I was the target. Not only that, but I would also be the last one chosen for any school activity. This reinforced my false belief and established a victim mindset within me. I lived in constant torment wondering what I would face. If the teachers tried to intervene, they were lied to. As soon as the teachers would walk away, the bullying would continue. This caused my traumatic view of getting involved with team sports and activities; it destroyed any remaining confidence I had in my abilities.

I will be the first one to admit that I did not do everything right. I did not know how to handle the bullying and I reacted by acting like a tattle-tale. I assume this led to the bullying intensifying; however, I just wanted justice. I hated being mistreated and needed protection.

This bullying led three young men to sexually molest me at least twice. One day, three young men cornered me in a hallway and pushed me into the side of the wall at my junior high school. They proceeded to touch my genital area. Being physically weaker, I could not push them away and they forced themselves onto me. I do not recall the entire ordeal, but after this trauma, all I remember was feeling very afraid of men. I instantly went to one of my teachers, reporting to them what had happened. The teacher pulled the boys into his office with me and asked them if they had done this. They confirmed that they had. All I remember is the teacher warning them that this was sexual assault and not to do it again. A few days later, they tried it again. I went to my teacher again. This time, his reaction was different. He told me he was unable to protect me and that I had to learn to stand up for myself. I felt powerless! The bullying continued throughout the rest of my school days. It was not until years later that I realized what transpired.

When I left school, I thought my days of bullying were done, but it followed me into the workplace. There were many occasions where employees and managers alike would gang up on me. No matter what I did, I never got any justice for what was willfully done to me. I was consistently painted as the troublemaker, not the victim. I was told I deserved this treatment, and this adversely affected my work performance. It was the same vicious circle wherever I worked. I would be faced with countless false allegations. People would twist their narrative about me, and I would live in so much fear, that I could not rise above the bullying to report it. Or, if I did report my side of the story, I was looked at like the one who was wrong.

Earlier, I shared the story of the gentleman who defrauded me financially. When I discussed the issue with his minister, who was a mutual acquaintance, it seemed it would be the first time in my life I would get justice. The minister quickly dealt with the issue, ordering him to pay up or face consequences and gave him a deadline to do so. The couple agreed that they would do whatever it took to make it right. They did not do it, so I took them to small claims court, getting a judgement in my favor. On several occasions, he said he had, or would send, the money but did not. I also received numerous emails from this gentleman, which I felt were threatening and bullying. He sent emails using aliases pretending to be a lawyer or a police officer, spinning the narrative against me. When I shared these emails with the minister, I was told he was too busy to deal with this situation, telling me to go to the police. He seemed to absolve himself of the behavior of his church member, leaving me devastated.

It left me feeling I would never get the justice owed to me.

Bullying has that effect on victims. A victim is silenced into submission and the bully gets to do what they want. No wonder most victims of abuse and bullying do not report it. They feel their voice will not be heard. It is times like this that victims need an advocate.

Why do bullies and abusers get away with their behaviors? They love to instill fear into their victims. However, it is a projection of their own insecurities and fears. They do not feel they are enough, so they need to find someone they can attack to give them a sense of satisfaction. Bullies love to project a sense of power over their victims. They want their victims powerless and to live in fear of them. They have a sense of fear and inadequacy and want to reinforce their ring of power.

If a person goes through bullying in their life without assistance or support, they will live in a state of constant torment. Usually, victims of bullying become very submissive and compliant people. They have lived their lives following the rules and never learned to take a risk in life due to the deep-seated fear they live under. They will not risk rejection; they live under clouds of shame and see themselves as the problem. At the very root of the behavior, is an overarching fear. Those who have been wounded by abuse and bullying may never acknowledge that their motivation and behaviors stem from fear, as they have been so used to being shut down emotionally by others or even worse, ignored.

In my case, bullying almost led me to suicide. Suicidal thoughts permeated my mind frequently until I got the help I needed. Sometimes, I felt it was my only escape from the raging effects of bullying on my life. Over the years, the emotional scars of the bullying have healed slowly, but I still wrestle with thoughts that I may be bullied every time I face new situations. The residue of what I faced still affects my decisions and I must make a conscious effort not to succumb to fear.

In 2 Corinthians, Paul the Apostle instructs the church at Corinth that, "We destroy arguments and every lofty opinion raised against the knowledge of God, and take every thought captive to obey Christ." (2 Corinthians 10:5, ESV) What does Paul mean by that?

I believe this scripture implies that the more we take our thoughts captive and filter them through Christ, the more we can recognize God's thoughts toward us. We will be able to intercept the negative thoughts and recognize their source. We all want to be liked and valued, as we were created for acceptance and love. Anyone who tells you otherwise is lying to you and themselves. I have learned much about standing up to bullying, but my greatest weapon has been forgiveness. Forgiveness does not excuse and justify the behaviors or actions of bullying. It removes its controlling influence. God can completely heal us from the pain of bullying.

We may remember the events, but the painful memories will not affect us.

Bullying can leave a massive open door to fear in our life if we allow it. It can leave an indelible grip of powerlessness and hopeless feelings of despair. It can prevent us from taking chances and opportunities, leaving us to live a safe life, instead of enjoying an abundant life of joy, peace, and love.

Bullying will leave us second-guessing everyone's motives, leaving us in a place of isolation, because we do not want to rise above the effects of it. Fear, through bullying, becomes a self-imposed prison of loneliness. Unless we deal with the roots of bullying, we will never live life to the fullest. We will either become depressed or we will become inwardly angry.

Having faced my past, I chose to reconnect with people I knew from my childhood. Doing this helped me gain a new perspective of the issues I had faced. I also discovered where many of my childhood peers and teachers ended up, including the homeroom teacher who allowed the sexual abuse to go unchecked.

I also chose to drive through the area from time to time. Each time I did, more of the pain from my childhood years surfaced and many times, the emotions would flood my mind. Each time they did, I chose to forgive those involved as the thoughts would come to my memory. God was at work in my heart starting to bring closure to the chaos. Yet, I never felt a total closure. There seemed to be a drawing inside of me that God wanted me to face the people that allowed the abuse.

In early 2012, I was driving back from Westlock, a rural Alberta town, and found myself near my old junior high. Just then, I felt the gentle whisper of God tug at my heart to drop by the school. I had no idea what was about to happen, and this decision changed my life forever. I had not walked into that school since I was a teenager. My heart started to beat uncontrollably, as I contemplated my decision. Fear rose in my heart but at the same time, supernatural peace, courage, and curiosity was rising in my inner being. I pondered what I would do or say should I decide to cross the threshold. With fear pounding through my being, I chose to walk through the doors.

Upon entering the school, I found myself in the office and received a friendly greeting from the secretary. I confidently told the secretary that I was a former student at the school and asked if it would be possible to say hi to some of the teachers that I happened to know that were still on staff. The secretary asked me the names of the teachers. Just then, my old homeroom teacher happened to walk past me. He intently looked at me and remarked that I looked familiar. Suddenly, he clued into my identity and called me by my name. I acknowledged that, indeed, it was me. Suddenly, he went white as a ghost. He stammered something to the effect of not being the person he was many years prior.

Then, my old principal walked out of his office and greeted me warmly. He was so happy to see me after all the years and asked what I had been up to. I was able to share with him my life journey and what brought me by that day. We walked through the school and he told me about the many changes that happened over the years since I last saw him. He was shocked by the transformation in my life. I was able to share with him about how I was being used in ministry and a bit of my healing journey. Then, he took me to the gym where one of my old classmates was teaching a class. Suddenly, fear gripped my heart. I realized I was about to face the fear that plagued my mind for years.

I saw my old classmate who now taught at the school. We had not seen each other since we were teens. She was shocked, bewildered, but overall happy to see me. She proceeded to introduce me to her class. All of a sudden, my mind started to flood with painful memories. I found myself looking down the hallway that led to the boys change room where the physical abuse happened.

I heard myself whisper, "I forgive every single person who ever abused me here." That moment, the darkness of my school days lifted, and my heart felt free. Fear lost its grip on my heart and mind. I had clarity, and the love of God filled my heart. Freedom flooded my heart with waves of supernatural peace. This encounter brought me into a supernatural closure, resulting in a major victory.

Afterwards, the principal gave me the liberty to walk around and I happened to come across my math teacher. He was happy to see me after all the years and we exchanged email addresses. He, like others, had wondered what had happened to me and I was able to share a bit of my journey.

When I walked out of the school that day, I realized I had received closure. It was as if a cloud that had been over my mind for years had lifted. Right then, I had a supernatural flash of insight.

"When exposed to the light of God's revelation, fear will lose its hold on our hearts as we respond to God. We do not have to be a slave to a spirit of fear. We can have a sound mind and supernatural peace in our hearts."

From that day forward, I could freely drive through the Edmonton region without fear. Deep down inside, I knew although I would not live there again, I had achieved a major victory in my life, and I was experiencing a restoration of my childhood. Over the next several years, I continued to reconnect with teachers and classmates… some regularly. I never would have expected that.

One of my greatest experiences over the last while was reconnecting with a childhood friend from Grade 5 through Grade 8. I reached out to her on Facebook one day and she wrote me back, remembering me from years prior. We rekindled our friendship. In my school days, we had a special connection. She had deep compassion towards me. Her kindness helped keep me grounded and stable through my pain. She felt helpless to stop the bullying. At the same time, she still took a genuine interest in me and on occasion, she would walk home with me, making me feel safe and secure.

We talked about our childhood memories and throughout our discussions, I thought it would be something special if we could meet up for a dinner one night and see each other again. She thought it was a great idea and we made plans. Little did I realize that the very tools that God gave me on my healing journey were about to help this childhood friend. That night became one of the most special reconnections I faced, as we enjoyed several hours together. We spent hours talking about what I had faced and then she told me her story of what she faced. Through our discussion, I was able to share how God brought deep healing to my heart and closure. She was shocked by how I had allowed God to transform my life. Then, she dropped a bombshell and opened her life to me. She shared that her first husband left her due to an affair and how she lost friends because of it. That conversation allowed me to give her some Godly tools that would help her on her journey.

My friend and I still talk regularly, and we try to reconnect in person when time allows. Having her back in my life has been one of the most precious gifts I have received in this last season. It validated the healing journey I have been on and it showed me that God can redeem our lives out of the most difficult of situations.

Abuse & Bullying

Recently, I had a friend from my childhood church youth group die from brain cancer. I had managed to spend several visits with him and his family, having not seen them since I was fourteen. They were grateful for me making several visits to the hospital and requested that I speak at the funeral. That day, I spoke with confidence and boldness that they had never seen. After speaking at the funeral, I was able to see with fresh eyes how my childhood impacted many people around me. It was there that I began to realize that not everyone had bullied me. There were some people who cared deeply for me from my old church. I was able to connect with those people and they saw a huge change in who I was and who I had become.

That fall, I was invited to celebrate one of my youth leader's 60th birthday. It was a surprise party and his wife looked for volunteers to speak. Again, I volunteered to speak and that day, I caught my old youth leader by surprise. He told everyone after I spoke that I used to be this shy, quiet young man and now I was this bold, confident preacher. It was at that celebration, I realized God can profoundly change how we are seen if we invite Him into our process.

I want to end this chapter with hope. If we allow God to take us into our healing journey, God will surprise us. He can heal our brokenness and bring a tremendous testimony in and through our lives. If we respond to His gentle voice in our hearts, we will emerge transformed by His love, and people will be able to see it. It is not an easy choice to make, but I have found if we trust the Lord, He will bring us into a place of closure.

It will not deny that the events have happened, but it will bring closure and peace to our hearts. We will perceive His invisible hand that has continuously guided our lives.

Have you faced bullying or abuse in your life? You are not alone. God does not want you to be a victim of those situations. He wants to heal your heart from bullying and abuse, and from the victimization and helplessness you feel. Invite Him today into that process. He wants to give you healthy relationships that will bring value to your life. I am coming out on the other side of this in my life and learning to trust at a whole new level. You will, too, as you heal. Let Jesus, the friend that sticks closer than a brother, minister to you now. Believe that He will bring people into your life. He will not bully you, but walk with you on your journey.

7

Rejections

Rejection partners with fear to destroy people's lives. Both play off of each other. If not dealt with, rejection will devastate people's thinking. This will lead people down paths into even greater fear and destruction.

Rejection was never in God's original intent for our lives. Humans were created for relationships, acceptance, and love. It was God's original intent for us to be born into a family that would portray acceptance and love for one another. Simultaneously, the family unit would provide guidance in how to interact relationally. At the head of the home would be a father and mother who would help us adjust to life, while providing the protection, nurture, and guidance we all need. Our siblings would teach us how to relate on a social level with people our age and ideally, build lasting loving relationships. This does not always play out the way we would hope.

Late last year, I was invited by a friend to attend a baby dedication at a church I attended for several years. Again, I felt the gentle whisper of God's Spirit. He invited me to attend and it was at this service I faced down another fear. How would I cope with going back to a place where I had been rejected deeply? Let me take you on a little journey.

When I first attended this church, I found it challenging to break into peer relationships. It felt like it was virtually impossible to get to know anyone in the young adult community. Many of the young adults in the congregation were several years younger than me and were either dating or married. I felt out of place, as a slightly older, single young adult.

While attending this church, the finger of God was at work in my life, assisting me through the beginning stages of my healing process. I made headway in the church and eventually managed to befriend some people. I was welcomed into their group and enjoyed great times of fellowship.

A few years had passed. Since young adults were a significant demographic of the church, the senior pastor hired a newly married young adult pastor. From the first day we met, we did not see eye to eye. There were cultural differences and whenever I was around this young man, I felt like a second-rate person. I could not relate to his direct, straightforward personality, especially when he took issue that I was neither married or in a relationship. This led me to face one of the largest rejections I ever encountered.

Rejections

I was asked to co-lead the junior high youth ministry with two other people outside of his authority. For the first while, things were going smoothly. But then, on occasion, this minister would pester me for not being married or not having a girlfriend. He questioned if there were issues with me and belittled me saying things such as, "Don't get offended when people leave you out." I felt like he was putting a wedge between me and others in the young adult community. I repeatedly pushed him away, telling him I was not looking for anyone at the time. I was healing from my childhood trauma. Other times, he questioned where I got my teaching material from for the junior high group. I could not figure out why he was concerned with this. I had not taught anything that was contrary to the church's values or theology. It was none of his business!

This resulted with me being treated as the behind-the-scenes person with the young adult group and if I got close to anyone, I was pushed out of the way by him. I felt that this was not fair, and it was apparent he did not want me influencing others.

One night, I arrived early for my junior high evening and was busy preparing. He cornered me and demanded to have a private meeting immediately. I told him I was busy setting up for the evening and he told me that I would have to do my work later. This meeting was more important. In that meeting, I was falsely accused of having women issues in my life and that I secretly wanted to be in a dating relationship with certain females in the group. When I denied it, he proceeded to call me a liar, and told me I was no longer welcomed to be part of the young adult group.

He told me to keep the meeting private, as he had been given full permission to do whatever he wanted with me.

I felt like a deer caught in the headlights of an oncoming car. I went pale and fear gripped my heart. After he walked away, I collapsed into a pool of tears and thought I was spiraling out of control. A cloud of confusion gripped my mind. That evening, I do not know how I got through my lesson, and when I got home, I was emotionally exhausted. My parents were irate at the events. After discussing the issue thoroughly, my parents and I could not agree on a solution.

Overnight, my relational life went downhill at the church. I felt like I had lost over 90% of my friends and people avoided me like I had leprosy. Over nine months, I could not overcome the heaviness I felt over my life every time I would enter the building. When I would leave, I would be in tears wondering when I would feel normal again.

Finally one day, I cried out to the Lord wondering what I should do. I did not want to leave offended, but I knew nothing would change. I heard the gentle whisper that has always guided me so faithfully. The whisper was clear. "They will never see you differently. It's time to leave, son." I drove away in tears, knowing my season at that church was over. God released me. It was still hard to leave because I had hoped for restoration.

Rejections

That rejection was hard to take and it was out of it, that God birthed a very public prophetic ministry that had been prophesied over me years earlier.

I did not hear from anyone from that church for a long time. But slowly, certain people came back. They proceeded to tell me what was spoken behind my back. They realized what was being said about me was not in my character.

Four years after leaving this church, my friend, Pastor Bryan Logan, invited me to visit his church one Sunday. He was aware of what I had faced in my life in that previous season. After the Sunday morning service, he invited the young adults who had been impacted by my life to come to pray over me. That day, the front of the church was filled with young adults praying for God's healing and blessing over my life. I was in tears and could hear the voice of God so clearly whisper to my heart again, "This is the restoration of what was stolen from you by the other group of young adults." The security and love melted the rejection away like a fresh spring breeze melting snow.

In 2019, Bryan invited me to speak at a young adult camp with him. I was led to share my journey into the "Father Heart of God" and overcoming brokenness. It was at that camp; I realized the deep transformation and healing God had worked into my life. I shared confidently and boldly of God's work in my life. Bryan felt God was developing a powerful message that needed to be released. It was a highlight of my year and many young adults attending came to me afterward sharing how they were impacted by my vulnerability.

This culminated with the invite to attend a baby dedication at the former church. I thought I dealt with my heart after leaving the church, but I realized to get closure on the former season, I needed to return. The thought of this frightened me. But I knew God had invited me into the process and once again, I saw God's hand at work. When I walked through the doors of the church, the first two people who greeted me were two of my former junior high students who were now young adults. They had not seen me since I left the church, and they were so thrilled to see me again.

The next two people that greeted me were the senior pastor and a board member. They also were happy to see me. Afterwards, several others approached me. Slowly, I felt the buried rejection and fear slipping off of my heart. When I sat in the auditorium, I stayed towards the back, as I did not want to be noticed by people. However, I could not hide. People recognized me and came by to greet me. By the time the worship service started, I was able to sing the songs with a free heart. During that time, I felt like the last tentacles of rejection from that season lost their hold on my life.

After the service ended, I felt I had secured victory in my heart. Though I knew I was not called back to the church, the pastor told me that I was always welcome to visit. Right then and there, I knew God brought me closure.

Rejection is a deadly emotion if it is not dealt with internally. It contributes to people living in fear of others. People who live in rejection are very aware of the fear in their lives and have become accustomed to its negative effects. To feel safe and protected, people will build invisible walls of rejection in their hearts and minds. Rejection becomes a fortress in people's lives. No one can penetrate it, nor do they want to leave it.

Why do we face rejection? Perhaps, we are accustomed to not measuring up to other's expectations of what they want us to be. Or we are not the right height, weight, not smart in certain subjects, we have the wrong look, we do not have enough money, we have too much money, we do not have the right qualifications, or we are overqualified. Rejection comes from a wide variety of sources and unless we deal with and overcome the crushing disappointment that comes with rejection, we will remain crippled by its effects on our life.

We were not meant to live by the crushing power of rejection because we were designed for acceptance and love. We were created perfectly in God's image and God considers that image good. It is humans that have marred God's perfection. Perfection does not mean flawless. Perfection from the Greek is translated as "mature and complete". We all have flaws and when we live out of a rejected spirit, we try to hide those flaws. The flaws in our personality shine with God's glory in our lives. Each of the flaws reflects a different aspect of His grace in our lives and we can shine beautifully in our broken state, like light shining off a flawed diamond.

When our families of origin do not reflect acceptance and love, we tend to search after counterfeit attractions. It is not until God wrestles us down like Jacob and heals the broken heart that we can surrender to His healing. God loves to woo us gently from the places of rejection into healing. He wants our hearts foremost. Until our heart is healed from rejection, we cannot see clearly. God wants His love to be so secured in our hearts that nothing can separate us from that love. His love confronts the unhealed rejected areas of the heart to show us His lovingkindness and mercy in our brokenness. No position, possession, person, place, poverty, or prosperity can define us. Only God's love can fill the void of rejection. So often, we use 'things' to fill the void of rejection that we feel.

How many times have we filled our need for acceptance through getting the latest clothing fashions from our local clothing store? How many times have we bought a new car to keep up with our neighbors because they purchased one? How many times have we racked ourselves up in debt just because we had needed something to define ourselves outside of God's love to soothe our rejection? There are countless times that we have tried to fill the void that rejection has brought into our lives. I am not saying it is bad to drive a luxury car or wear beautiful clothing. I am not advocating a poverty spirit that glorifies being and looking poor. We need to define our identity through God's unconditional love, not rejection. For years, the Church has glorified poverty as Godliness. There is

Rejections

nothing Godly about being poor. Poverty has to do with a lack of resources, but it also has to do with rejection and a fear of lack.

How can poverty be a fear of lack and rejection? Simply put, we do not offer ourselves up for opportunities, as we do not believe we have what it takes to be successful. We expect to be rejected and never take chances that will improve our lives or go for opportunities that present themselves to us. We have low expectations of what we think we can accomplish and end up acting like chickens pecking out an existence, instead of soaring like an eagle on a wind thermal, enjoying the updrafts of life in the skies of unlimited potential. As we make choices to overcome the fear of rejection and poverty, we will exceed our wildest dreams.

When a person lives under rejection for long seasons, they can become critical. If it is not dealt with in a healthy manner, rejection manifests in anger. Anger can be channeled towards God and anger towards others. There are many accounts of buried rejection that people have carried for years that resulted in an explosion of anger. We were not designed to live in rejection. It was never God's intention. He intended that we would give and receive unconditional love. Love has the power to heal the wounds of rejection. When a person feels unconditionally loved and accepted, the wounds of rejection can be healed.

God's love is a healing balm. The love of God can reach into the very crevices of our hearts, melting the stone-cold feelings of hatred and being unloved, to tenderizing it like meat. Its relentless pursuit melts the winter of rejection and can bring us into a springtime of enjoying our lives in rich ways. As we learn our identity as loved sons and daughters of God, the grip rejection held will slide away and we will embrace our true birthright. We will learn to give away love. Instead of living imprisoned in a castle of fear surrounded by moats and the crocodiles, we will emerge from our fortress of solitude and enjoy a childlike abundant life. We will not see through the cracked lenses of rejection believing that all people see is the cracks and fissures of our failure. We will not want to hide them, but we will be able to embrace them and let the glory of God and the love of God shine through those areas, reflecting the glory that is within us.

This love will change the very countenance on our face and reflect on how and what we believe in our hearts about ourselves and others. Out of the abundance of our hearts will come rivers of love, encouragement, joy, and hope in the abundant life of Christ instead of bitterness, self-loathing, isolation, and fear. The fear of rejection that sealed our death warrant, will be displaced with a new innocence of the heart and a new acceptance of ourselves and others. We will be willing to take chances on new opportunities that present themselves and embrace with fresh confidence that we are not defined and chained to the past rejections. With the stronghold of rejection broken, we will live in a new dimension of living free from fear, able to bring the heart of God to the world around us. We will be able to see a world of color, instead of a world of black and white, and our relationships with people will be transformed in ways that we cannot even imagine.

Rejections

We must get healed from rejection. If not, we will carry the wounds of rejection and project it everywhere we go and live in caves of fear. It is subtle as we are usually blind to behaviors that have become ingrained in our personality, due to rejection. Unhealed rejection will cause us hold to ourselves in a spiritual prison. It will keep us trapped internally and prevent others from aiding us. When a person carries rejection in their spirit and they minister, they will see through cracked lenses.

Seasoned prophet Bob Jones has mentioned frequently that a person who carries a prophetic gifting is highly susceptible to rejection. Satan loves to wound individuals carrying a prophetic heart. The master plan is to get them to operate under a spirit of rejection. If unhealed, rejection will cripple a person with the bitterness of soul and heart. People that always see themselves as rejected will act out of a wounded spirit. The wounded spirit can fester into identity issues. When rejection runs unchecked, a 'poor me' mentality can develop. It will seek out to do anything to get acceptance. If unchecked, anger can develop in the personality towards the world, carrying a 'chip on our shoulders'. This will negatively affect the prophetic person and their message.

Unhealed, wounded prophetic people will tend to withdraw from the community and life, causing them to live in fear. When this happens, they can be prone to attacks on their life. There are times prophetic people need to be alone with God to hear what God is saying, but they were not created to be alone all the time. They must choose to reconnect with their community, or they risk becoming socially disengaged. It was never God's intention for the prophetically wired person to act like a monk hiding out alone in a monastery. It was His intention for the prophetic person to live in the community with every other gifting in the Body.

At the same time, the community of faith needs to be accepting and receptive of the prophetic person. If the community of faith fails to recognize or honor the gift, it will cause a prophetically wired person to pit themselves against the people to where they are called. They will perceive them as the "against me mentality" and become overly critical of the Body. When that happens, rejection can pervert their gift mix until the rejection is identified and healed. The person can develop a hard heart towards any kind of correction or emotional healing. An apostolic leader can translate the uniqueness of prophetic giftings, bringing a practical application to what the prophetic person has been shown. They can help bring clarity to the Body, helping the Body understand the uniqueness of the prophetic heart, while encouraging the Body to receive that person.

Unhealed rejection and fear can control a person's behavior. If not dealt with, a person can begin to live in paranoia, thinking everyone is out to get them. They may view people as a potential threat and fear will begin to subtly control their environment and the people in it. The people in that environment will be so tightly gripped by fear that they will take rejection on as well. This web of deception will seek to protect and control everything and everyone in that bubble, viewing anyone who approaches or disrupts that bubble as a threat, or suspicious, and lash out. They fail to realize the disruptor might have been sent to them to help. They

Rejections

unintentionally wound that messenger. The subtleness is that the person living in the fear and rejection will view themselves as right and the other person as a threat.

Have you battled rejection in your life? Consider talking with a Holy Spirit-filled counselor or a psychologist to explore how rejection has affected you. Also, take a moment right now to invite Jesus and Holy Spirit into the wounds of rejection you have faced. He is near to the brokenhearted. Pray this aloud. "Holy Spirit, You are my counselor. I invite You to minister the acceptance of God to every place of rejection I have faced in my life. I ask You to root out every weed or seed of rejection in my life. Heal my mind of every thinking of rejection. Flood my mind and spirit with the truth of your acceptance. I receive by faith God's acceptance and God's perfect love into my rejected areas. Reveal to me how you and the Father see me and how I am accepted by you fully and completely and I am accepted in the Body of Christ. I choose to see myself as accepted into God's beloved family. Amen."

8

Perfectionism

Christian perfection has been a highly debated discussion for years in the Body of Christ. There are varied schools of thought that have come through the Body of Christ about *perfectionism*. Most notably was a booklet written by John Wesley entitled: *A Plain Account of Christian Perfection*[ix]. Throughout the years, the Body of Christ has wrestled with the finished work of Christ at the Cross and perfectionism. Are we perfect the moment we accept Christ's finished work at the Cross? Or, are we in the process still? Is perfection a work of grace and faith, or is it about our works, too? Do we ever attain a state of perfection here while we are living? Theologians have wrestled with this topic for years.

When initially looking at the word translated "perfect" from the Greek, the word used is *teleios*. *Teleios* means to be brought to its end, full-grown, mature, or to be complete. Perfect in the English has several meanings and one that most people use is flawless, or completely free of faults or defects. We can use the English definition of "perfect" to define the finished work of Jesus at the Cross. But if we build upon the Greek, we will have a more complete understanding of *teleios*.

The incorrect application of the word "perfect" has led believers to live in fear of perfectionism. This fear can lead to deep-seated rejection of others. Paul writes to the Galatian church that "it was for freedom Christ has set us free and that we are no longer to be in bondage to a yoke of slavery." (Galatians 5:1, my paraphrase) When we overemphasize an incomplete definition of perfection, we fall into its trap. Self-perfectionism is rooted in fear and has ensnared people making them feel unless their behavior is flawless or fault-free, they disqualify themselves from the promises of God. The promises of God are not rooted in our flawless self-perfectionism. The promises of God are rooted in faith in the living Word of God and God Himself.

Jesus is the only perfect God-man. He is fully man and yet fully God. His sinless perfection fulfills the prophet's declarations and the full requirements of the Mosaic law. We can rest in the fact that we are not disqualified by performance. We are not slaves to a God who is holding us over hell, waiting to throw us into eternal torment. Rather, we are sons and daughters of a loving Father who sent His perfect Son to die in our place, so that we could be adopted into His family. Much fear-based theology has come through the Greek mindset of God that we need to appease God with our works. That thinking is rooted in a fear-based perfectionism. Love motivates us in Holy Spirit-led good works towards others. It stems from the love God gave us in our hearts when we accepted Jesus as our Savior and our Lord.

Our perfection is best defined by the word *teleios* not as flawless or faultless, as we all still sin even after receiving Jesus as our Lord and Savior. We are seen through Jesus as faultless and flawless, free of all defects because we have received the righteousness of Christ. The God kind of righteousness allows us to become fully grown and mature sons, while we are being shaped and conformed into that image.

When we live in a state of false perfectionism, we live as fear-based people always trying to disqualify ourselves and others from our image. This kind of perfectionism, at its roots, is a behavior issue of not feeling that we measure up to others' standards. If we just do better or get better grades at school or work, we will finally get our acceptance. It is a striving after the wind. There will always be someone smarter than us or stronger than us. If we live through the cracked lens of perfectionism, we erroneously conclude that no one will ever be good enough. We will live insecurely, unable to commit to others in a relationship, because they might be better than ourselves or we might not be good enough for them. We end up erecting walls of rejection, a form of self-protection.

When Japan started to mass produce cars, they were made of ill-prepared metals. The cars rusted out prematurely compared to the mechanical components. They were manufactured well but the metals used in their building were not prepared for the various climates in which they would be used. As the Japanese car market started to ramp up, they realized that they needed to improve the metal treatment to prevent premature rusting.

From 1983-1989, Toyota invested over a billion dollars to develop the *Lexus* brand. They made over 450 prototypes and had many engineering teams working on the Lexus project. The original look of the car was not an initial priority. The major priority was creating a dependable, quality vehicle that would supersede the build quality of the benchmark luxury sedan of that era, the Mercedes Benz S-Class. Mercedes Benz had domineered the automotive luxury industry for years. Toyota wanted to dominate the luxury industry, dethrone Mercedes Benz, and created a whole new brand image through the Lexus brand. Believe it or not, Toyota initially manufactured sewing machines, which helped shape their corporate philosophy of making a precision-made vehicle. Mercedes Benz had been the first patented vehicle.

To show their dominance, Lexus's first marketing campaign, "Balance,"[x] was devised to demonstrate how smooth the engine ran on their LS. They proceeded to set a pyramid of champagne glasses on their LS sedan and put the car on a dyno, taking the car up to speeds of 145 miles per hour/230 kilometers per hour and back down to zero. It was so smooth that the glasses did not break or fall off. Their goal with their sedan was to create a quiet, smooth ride in which people could have a normal conversation at autobahn speeds.

Perfectionism

How do the Japanese car market and perfection intertwine? The initial marketing slogan of Lexus was "The Relentless Pursuit of Perfection."[xi] The Japanese wanted to engineer the perfect car. At the core of Japanese culture is a personal responsibility for failure. Once the Lexus car came out into the market, there was a potential flaw with the cruise control and a brake light housing. Instead of hiding minor flaws like other auto manufacturers had done, they exposed it to the market and recalled every single vehicle that had been sold. Lexus covered the cost of the repairs. This could have crippled a new brand like Lexus; however, when they fixed the defects, the dealers servicing the cars were instructed to return the cars gas-filled, and the cars washed and detailed. This left the customers ecstatic and very loyal to this brand. Lexus has emerged as one of the highest rated, best-selling, and recognized luxury brands in the world since that time. Their commitment to quality, continuous improvement, and customer service has been recognized worldwide.

Lexus is a Japanese car manufacturer who wanted their cars to be perfect. They could not let their car be seen with any kind of fault, as the Japanese feared losing face. I have observed that Japanese culture does not want to face shame in any way. They incorporated this thinking into their car manufacturing process.

Some students strive to get straight A's for their parents. If they can get a straight-A report card, they feel perfect and accepted. If they fail or get anything lower than A's, they believe they will not get into an Ivy League school. If they do not get into the school, they believe they would not get recognized by corporate America and get the job that could make their parents proud of them. When reading the job descriptions in today's job market, I have observed that companies tend to write unrealistic postings with the expectation to hire only the best of the best, and if you do not meet the qualifications, your chances of being hired are slim.

How about the woman who desperately wants to be married, while carrying unhealed roots of perfectionism? She might meet many potential spiritually healthy men who present themselves, but because she has this root in her life, she subconsciously blocks them. This woman will end up lonely wondering why she never could marry, not realizing it was her fear of making a wrong choice that was holding her back. The delusion of her perfectionism makes her strive after unrealistic men that only exist in fantasy. How many women do you see that want their husband to have the looks of Brad Pitt, the money of Bill Gates, and the faith of Jesus Christ Himself? We are all a work in progress and if we strive after the fantasy of Hollywood perfectionism, we will never accept the realist view that we are all being shaped into the image of Jesus Christ. This is not an endorsement for young women to date any man. A good man needs emotional wholeness and maturity before getting romantically involved with a woman. He needs to be mature to not stir up love until love so desires, and to be willing to look at the imperfections of others and see how he can help bring strength and cover imperfections.

Think about a young man who has a great business idea. His perfectionism makes him fearful of making mistakes and he never starts the

Perfectionism

business he has a great passion to begin. He could feel he has to wait for perfect conditions before stepping out. He can become miserable because he may end up working for others' dreams, while he watches others achieve their goals. His fear can misdirect him to miss the opportunity and abort the opportunities presented to him. We need to take the steps and a path will start to appear. We do not need to see the result; we must be willing to take the initial steps needed by faith, trusting in God who will perfect it all.

Perfectionism is a cruel tyrant. It holds us captive to fear, slavery, and indecision. If we wait passively, we will watch others seize opportunities, while we stay in our prisons of hopelessness and despair, wondering why life is passing us by and no one has taken us up on opportunities. Waiting does not have to be passive. It can be actively looking at opportunities, and prayerfully taking an examination of each one. But at the root, perfectionism will prevent us from seeing the right opportunity when it stares us in the face. Perfectionism can so easily and subtly lie to us stating that we need to wait for something better; that the opportunity is not what we want. However, if we wait for perfect, flawless, faultless conditions, we may never move.

If you ever watched the movie *Indiana Jones and the Last Crusade*,[xii] you may remember the scene where Indiana Jones comes to a place where he must take a leap of faith. There is no visible path to the other side of a great chasm. But he has a diary in his possession from his father. He must believe that this diary contains accurate information on how to cross the bottomless chasm. Once he takes his step of faith from the lion's head, the invisible pathway appears before him, and he can safely cross the impassable abyss. Likewise, we must press passed our fears when things look impossible and take steps of faith. Only then do we see miracles happen.

Have you ever observed the turtle? Turtles cannot move unless they first stick their necks out. Once they stick their necks out, the legs extend, and a turtle can walk. Consider emulating this in your life. When we choose to take a risk, we can start making progress in our own lives. If we keep our necks in, we risk never entering the fulfillment of things we have wanted in life and may forfeit our destiny.

If we persist in our shell, we remain fearful and carry a survivalist lifestyle. God never intended this for us. If we do not deal with our fears, it can lead to depression or suicide. Often, perfectionism manifests as hopelessness, despair, or unrealistic expectations perpetuating low self-worth and self-esteem. Perfectionism can also lead us into overcontrolling our environments.

Perfectionism is very selfish and can ruin relationships. It is inward-focused, instead of focusing on the needs of others. When a person is rooted in perfectionism, they are unable to see how their behavior adversely affects others and their desire to fix everyone and every situation. Instead of focusing on the beauty of flaws, they cover them up as a self-defense mechanism from hurt or rejection. It is a shame-based behavior that can negatively affect every aspect of a person's personality and the relationships that surround them. People will tend to reject them. They feel they can never measure up to the standards set by the perfectionist, which leads them to grow embittered and take on roots of rejection in their own lives. Unless healed, a perfectionist will live in a bubble of fear their entire lives, not realizing how devastating the effects have been upon them and the others that are closest to them.

Our security and confidence cannot be rooted in our self-perfection. It must rest on God's perfection and not our own, as He is the only perfect one. He invites us and brings us into His perfection (*teleios*) as we are conformed more and more into His image in maturity. Yet we are never flawless, but in His sight we are. Our righteousness is seen as filthy rags, but He sees us clothed in Christ's righteousness and Christ's perfection, fully, unconditionally, and completely loved, Nothing can separate us from the unconditional love that He has lavished upon us. His love looks at our flaws and gives us beauty for our ashes and crowns us with His goodness. It is God's perfect, unrelenting love that casts out and displaces all fear and brings us into healthy confidence in God, in ourselves, and in our relationships. As we heal, we can boldly engage our world around us in confident assurance that His goodness is what we reflect. We do not have to be flawless and faultless to be mature, complete, or fully grown.

When perfectionism and fear control a life, the person will want everything to be faultless or flawless. The behavior will demand an unrealistic expectation of everyone in their lives. They will start to nitpick other's faults and flaws and will tell those in their bubble how others are imperfect, while covering their own flaws and faults. The perfectionist lives in delusion. They downplay their imperfections and hide from others' imperfections. The result: No one is good enough for the perfectionist's circle and they end up isolating themselves and their bubble from everyone. Those in that circle end up embracing low self-identity and live in a vicious circle of comparison, never feeling anyone can live up to their unrealistic standards.

What happened with Adam and Eve in the Garden? After eating the fruit from the tree of the knowledge of good and evil, they both realized they were both naked. They decided to hide from God in the Garden, as they judged themselves as imperfect in the sight of a perfect, holy God. They hid their flaws and mistakes from Him. It was right then and there that fear entered humanity.

My false perfectionism stemmed from an incorrect foundation of fear and comparing myself to others. This resulted in me striving to be perfect in everything I did. There were times I watched others get blessed with promises that I wanted, but I erroneously thought that I was not perfect or worthy enough to have what others bought or had. My false humility repeatedly lied to me, telling me I was not worthy enough, good enough, or perfect enough to get what others got freely. These lies spiraled me into a tailspin of despair.

While growing up, I watched my younger siblings excel in school leading me to struggle and wrestle with torment of why I faced immense

Perfectionism

difficulty in learning that came naturally for them. This resulted in comparison. When they would be at the top of the class, I felt like I needed to be perfect. They appeared to go after their dreams and goals without difficulty and they achieved them. When I pursued my goals, every door slammed in my face. This fueled the unworthiness I battled and put me in a state of despair, resulting in me spending years serving the dreams of everyone else. Internally, I came to realize I was struggling with my false perfectionism and did not know how to break free. I would not take chances, as I did not want to be rejected. I never sought out relationships with women, as I did not think I deserved to have a relationship.

I was ensnared by perfectionism and believed wrongly that by serving others, I thought I would be finally welcomed and given my dreams. I did not realize I was serving out of performance, instead of love. The more I served out of performance, the less acceptance I received, and the more I felt like a doormat. God gently exposed my heart to my self-deception and performance-based behavior. I would not achieve my goals by acting or being counterfeitly perfect. It would be trusting in God that would promote me. The more I learned about God's pure, relentless love for me, the perfectionism lost its grip on my thinking. God is still at work untangling my fear and the more I am healed in this area, the more I can freely embrace the unconditional love of God. It is the love of God that helps me relax in the presence of others and helps me overcome my social awkwardness.

God's truth reveals to us that we are fully acceptable for who we are, and we do not have to strive after everyone's approval and acceptance. Moreover, we do not have to be good or perfect at everything we do to be accepted by God or others. Our Heavenly Father accepts us and loves us for who we are. He created us in His image to reflect His glory and His presence to the world around us. There are many limitations that we might have, but we can choose to focus day by day on the strengths we have, as well as on His strength and thoughts. We do not need to dwell on our weaknesses, shortcomings, or imperfections, but we can embrace His perfection in our life and unconditional love. We are fearfully and wonderfully made in His image and He declares that image is good.

Do you battle with perfectionism in your life? Perhaps, take some time to journal how it has affected you. Welcome Holy Spirit into that area. Pray right now, "Holy Spirit, You already see me as the Father does. I repent for my striving and I choose to trust Your complete work, that You, who started this work, are faithful to complete it. You made me already perfect and You are conforming me daily to the Father's image. I choose to let go of striving; I choose to enter the rest of God. I ask You to heal my heart today. Let me freely receive Your grace and allow me to rest in Your unconditional love to wash away all performance and perfectionism. Amen." May God grant you the strength and courage as you discover how special you are in His eyes.

9
The Power of Forgiveness

We have examined the many areas of how fear controls our lives. We have also seen the different forms of fear that controlled my life and influenced my decisions. But there are antidotes for fear. We do not have to live as slaves to fear. Our birthright is freedom. Fear was never meant to master us. I have made much progress in my healing journey and for the next few chapters, I am going to explore tools that helped bring freedom to me from fear. These tools are by no means exhaustive, but they have helped me kickstart my healing journey.

One of the greatest tools I have incorporated is the power of forgiveness.

Forgiveness does not excuse or forget the behavior. It neutralizes the power of the behavior holding us captive. Forgiveness allows us to be free from the grips of the hurt. It is not reconciliation between the parties or the events, though that can be an outcome from choosing forgiveness. If we choose to walk in forgiveness, we can open the door to reconciliation, eventually. There is no impetus to seek reconciliation if the other party does not want to take responsibility for their actions or behaviors.

Choosing to forgive can be the most liberating thing a person can do to loosen fear's grip. When we choose to forgive, we choose to drop our hurt and choose to trust again. It does not mean we should blindly trust immediately, but it can set us on a journey of walking out of fear into freedom. The act of forgiveness invites us to trust others, even after people have done a great wrong to us. When we choose to forgive, we open ourselves up to the possibility that we will be hurt again. By forgiving, we can begin to trust God, other people, and ourselves again.

Earlier, I shared the story of a man who defrauded me financially. I did not share how the story ended. Upon winning the lawsuit, I tried to collect what was legally mine. Yet, I was harassed by the gentleman continuously. A spirit of fear was bombarding my mind daily from the actions of this man. During this time, two father-figures in my life approached me, exhorting me to forgive the man's actions. That infuriated me! At the same time, the thought wrestled me to my core. I wanted to be right; I wanted to be paid back what was owed to me; I wanted justice! The victim in me raged inside remembering the times I failed to get justice from all the years of deep hurt done to me from my school days to that current situation. I had no desire to show mercy to a person that had hurt me. Mercy felt like weakness and a cop-out, not a strength!

The Power of Forgiveness

The Lord used that conversation to prick my heart. The Lord gently whispered to me, "Son, will you let me pay this man's debt?" It was so gentle and loving that I could not ignore it. It haunted me for several days, as I contemplated my actions. When the Lord touches areas in our lives with His finger, He invites us into a great discovery of truth from His heart.

The more I reflected, the more I realized there was nothing and no one except God that would ever get this man to pay me back what he stole. The man had a heart of stone. But I had the choice of walking free from fear. This was no easy choice. I felt justified in my choice not to forgive. My mind was flooded with thoughts. "Why should I be the one always forgiving people for what they had done to me. No one had come back to me repenting for what they had done to me. It wasn't right then, and it wasn't right now! Was I meant to never have justice in my life?"

Inside the depth of my heart, I knew I would not be able to escape the finger of God pressing on my life. I also knew what could happen if I chose to forgive. I knew this person could interpret it as a sign of weakness and take advantage of my perceived weak state.

While pondering my decision, I consulted a father-figure in my life who had been deeply wronged in his life, to get his perspective. He gently reminded me that forgiveness was different from reconciliation. He also counseled me that he had seen the effects of the man's behavior on my life and that I had lost joy. The man's behaviors were now affecting and controlling my behavior. It was like a cloud of confusion, and fear was raging over my mind.

I finally took the plunge. I knew that I was never going to be paid back. Unless I forgave, I knew I would never become free of the fear that had gripped my heart. So, I called the courts to find out how to remove the legal judgment. The clerk I talked with was shocked that I wanted to remove the judgment, asking me if I had been paid back yet. Again, I asked the Lord for guidance and He instructed me to tell the clerk that an anonymous third party had agreed to pay the debt. The Lord assured me that He would look take care of me if I chose this path.

I told the clerk I had not been paid back, but an anonymous third party advised me that they were going to pay the man's debt. When pressed if I had the money in my bank account, I told them I had not been paid yet, but this person paying the debt was fully trustworthy and had never broken His word. The court clerk told me to draft a statement to indicate what I had declared. Upon receiving my statement, the court would release the judgment, warning me once they did, I gave up all legal rights to collect on the debt. With tears flooding my eyes, I wrote the statement out to the court and mailed it in. Once I did that, the cloud of fear and confusion left me. I still faced a long journey of trusting again, but it felt like a beginning.

After forgiving the debt, my financial struggles were not alleviated, but I managed to pay every bill on time and even though it meant I could not get the condominium or car I so desperately wanted, God took care of my needs. He was faithful to His Word.

When we choose forgiveness, we choose God's heart over our own perceived rights. Forgiveness is a choice we must make if we are ever to overcome fear in our life. If we choose forgiveness, the grip of fear loosens its hold over us, and any confusion that clouds our mind, or thinking, also drops off. The heart of mercy of our Heavenly Father is vastly deeper than the ocean. His relentless love chases down the fear in our hearts and reveals it, so we can heal.

Forgiveness is an offensive weapon against the enemy. When we choose to forgive people who have hurt us deeply, we partner with Heaven over our lives. The grace of God enters our fears when we forgive. This supernatural grace empowers us to overcome the fear that we have, displacing it and allowing us to walk in new measures of authenticity and trust towards others. When we have been hurt deeply, it is in our nature that we do not want to trust. A lack of trust is the breeding ground for fear to take root. We need to have trust in our lives. When we choose to live in suspicion and doubt, we are empowering fear to rule our minds and hearts and will view everyone as a threat to our lives in one way or another. When we choose to walk in forgiveness, we empower the love of God in our hearts and lives, welcoming and including people in that space. Fear constricts and restricts. Forgiveness accepts and trusts.

Have you ever felt like you are walking on eggshells in a certain relationship? When you are walking in fear in that relationship, feelings like that arise in the heart. Fear causes our defenses to rise. When you walk authentically, you can risk being vulnerable. When you walk in forgiveness and understanding, you can walk unguarded.

One of the mistakes I made in my life was trusting everyone immediately and taking them at face value. I am not suggesting you give your trust to just everyone and anyone and become best friends with them. That's foolishness. God wants to bring people into your life that you can trust and with whom you can work towards healing. Trust must be earned and when it is broken, forgiveness offers another chance for reconciliation between the parties. Broken relationships are never part of God's idea for us. God's idea has always been for us to walk together in a relationship with Him and others. If we find ourselves living like a warship, armed and ready to battle, we will never know what it is to walk in peace and harmony with ourselves and others. It usually means we have issues in our hearts that need to be healed. We are not to be people of war all the time, but people of peace, as Christ in us is peace. Forgiveness empowers the peace of God to rule and reign in our hearts. It allows love to freely flow.

Forgiveness places us in a vulnerable spot. This vulnerable spot is the tipping point where we make the choice to forgive. We can choose "fight or flight," or we can rest, relax, and heal. It is this place of vulnerability that God can overthrow mistrust in our hearts. We may feel very violated by the vulnerability, but our act of forgiveness will place us in rest.

Vulnerability is the place where true authenticity is fashioned and forged. When we find a place to trust, we can let our walls down and we can truly find the healing we are looking for. It is at this place we can start to flourish in our walks if we have been crippled by fear. It is our choice. God will never impose His will on us, but if we do not listen to His still small voice, we will rob ourselves of living our best life.

Forgiveness will help us gain authority to help others heal from their fears. If we choose to hold on to our fears, we will never rise to the fullness of what we could accomplish in God. The choice is ours to make. When God invites us into the places of fear, He does it for a greater purpose. It does not always appear that way when we are still in the situation. However, if we submit to the hand and the wheel of the master potter, He will shape us for His purposes that will exceed our wildest expectations. I know that I have experienced this in my forgiveness journey. I did not always want to face my fears, but in facing them, the Lord brought closure to past wounds that had previously crippled me.

When God invites us on His potter's wheel, it is an invitation for us to grow and allows God to bring us into maturity as His sons and daughters. When God's finger touches sensitive areas in our lives, our natural tendency is to get off the wheel. Facing forgiveness is not an easy choice by any stretch of the imagination. Forgiveness is the most selfless act we can ever do for ourselves and others. Instead of pointing the finger in judgment towards others, we allow God to have mercy on those who have wronged us. It is about laying down what we view as our rights and our needs, and trusting that God will fight our battles. If we choose to withhold forgiveness towards others, God will withhold from us. Eventually, it can sap the free-flowing presence of God within us, as well.

Jesus said that we are to ask God to "forgive us our debts, as we also have forgiven our debtors." (Matthew 6:12, ESV)

Later, in the Gospel of Matthew, in response to Peter's question to the number of times we should forgive, Jesus replied, "I do not say to you seven times, but seventy-seven times." (Matthew 18:22, ESV)

Lastly, Paul, the apostle, exhorted the church of Colossae that "if one has a complaint against another, forgiving each other; as the Lord has forgiven you, so you also must forgive." (Colossians 3:13, ESV)

These scriptures and numerous others throughout the New Testament emphasize forgiveness being a key component of our walk with our Lord.

The potter's wheel works on our hearts and allows the Lord to point out the issues in our lives and what we have done to others. He helps us see and deal with the wickedness of our own hearts and where we might have wronged others, intentionally or unintentionally.

We might not be able to acknowledge these easily, but there are times we have hurt others as much as others have hurt us. An acquaintance of mine once told me that unforgiveness is like drinking poison and expecting the other person to die. Unforgiveness undermines the work of God within us and can clog the pipeline of the Spirit of God in our lives. We were meant to be the conduit of God's love to those around us. We were never meant to punish those who hurt us. We are not the judge, jury, and executioner. We are meant to be the vessels of God's mercy to the world around us. Consider that, the next time someone deliberately wrongs you. Kenn Gill, my pastor, loves to share that it is better to be the one who has been wronged, than to be the one that does wrong to another. It is never easy being the one wronged, but if we know how to forgive, we will be in peace and joy.

Forgiveness is a powerful weapon that displaces fear in others. Think of Joseph's brothers. After Joseph was betrayed by his brothers, over thirteen years passed, and Joseph was serving as the Egyptian Pharaoh's second in command. When a famine had devastated the known world, Joseph's father, who thought Joseph was long dead, sent his brothers to get food in Egypt. When they faced Joseph, the Bible tells us that they did not recognize him and they bowed before him, fulfilling the dreams Joseph had as a 17-year-old, years earlier. (The dream had threatened his brothers.) At the end of the story, Joseph ends up revealing his true identity as their brother. Instead of living in fear of them, he embraced them and shared how God turned around their evil actions for the good of all. His selfless act of forgiveness, mercy, and love towards them displaced their fear, and as well turned the situation into a joyful family reunion.

They all ended up living blessed lives in Egypt, all fully cared for and were properly provided for.

I have found in my healing journey that God loves to show us how far we have come in our lives. I would have never guessed in my wildest dreams that as I made the choice to forgive, that I would be invited to speak about my life openly to young adults in the same region where I was wounded. Forgiveness truly works!

For years, I struggled with driving through the region where my abuse and bullying transpired. Now, I have been able to overcome the fear and pain in my own heart, and drive through the territory in freedom. Believe me, the grace of God is bigger than our fears. I have faced the fears down often and will continue to do so for the rest of my life. The emotional scars I have are still in my memory and the effects of what was done to me, still linger. Yet, the power of them does not cripple my thoughts and choices as much. There are times still that I feel apprehensive about situations. Those times, I have had to make a conscious choice to press passed the fear and choose forgiveness again. I may never have people repent and ask for forgiveness for what they did to me. I, however, made the choice to forgive and move on. The first one to forgive is usually the strongest. Choose forgiveness, it is the only sane choice to make if you do not want to be crippled by others and by fear anymore.

Forgiveness removes the fear scales off our eyes. Once the scales are removed, we can see people through clear lenses. Before I started healing,

The Power of Forgiveness

I believed that everyone was out to bully me. I just wanted to retreat into a cave of safety. That which I feared kept coming upon me everywhere I went.

The more I chose to forgive, the clearer I was enabled to view people through God's eyes. Believe me, this will be your experience, as well. It was a choice on my part to trust again and out of that trust, has come many tests to pick up stones of the offense again. But I am learning to drop them and stop acting like a victim to life. I am becoming a victor in life. The truth of God's Word sets us free in life. It is a lifelong journey; it is not easy. It is a process. But it will be worth it. Just take each step as it comes and soon, you will be able to run free where you used to walk with a limp.

There are excellent resources on the topic of forgiveness. One powerful book that I have read that helped me immensely was the book *Total Forgiveness*,[xiii] by R.T. Kendall. This book will wrestle with your heart if you choose to take the plunge into a healing journey. But you will come out on the other side stronger, and more emotionally whole, if you allow forgiveness to work into your wounds. Dr. Kendall has a gentle way of prodding at your heart if you open your life up to the Spirit of God working through you. He writes in a way that encourages you to drop your defenses. The book is not hard to read, very Biblically sound, yet practical at the same time.

Invite Holy Spirit right now to show you the people that you need to forgive. You can trust Him to reveal if reconciliation is needed. "Holy Spirit, I choose to fully forgive those people who hurt me. I choose to drop the rock of offense I have been carrying towards them. I ask You to bless them, I ask You to release them, and I choose to walk out of offense from what they have done. Father forgive them for they do not know what they did to me. I choose to give up my anger, my bitterness, and my need to be right. I choose to give these people back to You. Forgive me for anything I have done to hurt them, as well. Show me if I need to humble myself and seek reconciliation with these people. I release them into Your hand, and I choose to walk free from any pain and fear associated with these people. I surrender them all back to You and even if they do not seek reconciliation or forgiveness from me, I will no longer hold on to the fear or unforgiveness. Amen."

This will be a bit of a journey for you and as you choose to forgive, you will find many memories and emotions rising to the surface. Take time to process each person Holy Spirit brings to your memory. Do not be in a hurry. This is not a five-minute fix. Let God do a deep transforming work in your spirit towards each person. It might take days, weeks, or months to process forgiveness, but you can and will emerge victorious in this if you let the Lord have His way in this process. It will be liberating to your heart and you will see with fresh eyes, and your fear will dissipate.

10

All You Need is Love

Earlier, we explored the topic of perfectionism and how it can cause us to live fear-filled lives. Perfectionism causes us to avoid opening ourselves up to love. The Bible refers to God's love as perfect love and that His love casts out all fear.

Most cultures, including the Greek culture, held fear-based views towards the gods they let rule over them. They did not view the true God as loving Father. Their view of God was as one who was going to smite them for their shortcomings and failures, and they had to appease them. The head of all gods in Greek culture was Zeus, the Sky and Thunder god who ruled from Mount Olympus. The gods were at war with each other, at times, and there was a hierarchical structure to their order. They had human bodies, both good and evil, male and female. Each of them representing a facet of the human condition.

The Greek culture was polytheistic, meaning they worshiped multiple gods. The apostle Paul encountered this when he traveled to Athens. In Acts Chapter 17, when Paul walked around the city of Athens, he saw all the statues the Athenians had erected and how they worshipped them. Paul remarked about how devout and religious they were as a culture. The Athenians also made a statue to the unknown god to cover their bases. Paul used that as a point of reference to address the monotheistic view of the Hebrews. This allowed him to introduce the Greek culture to the Hebraic God as the one who created humanity in His image to love and to be loved, as His offspring. Paul tied it to some writings from Aratus,[xiv] the Greek poet from around 300 BC that we were his (referring to Zeus) offspring. It led him explaining to the Athenian's that they were Jehovah God's offspring.

The Hebraic culture holds a monotheistic view of God. God is one God and is the Creator of Heaven and Earth. Moses told the children of Israel, "Hear O Israel, The Lord our God, the Lord is one" (Deuteronomy 6:4, ESV) while describing God's nature. Hebraic culture was wrapped around the family, and faith was the cornerstone of the culture. Children were taught from an early age that Jehovah was a loving Father. Jehovah was interested in the affairs of their lives, which was in stark contrast to the Greek mindset. The Hebrews learned of the fear of the Lord, which was not terror, but a healthy love and respect for Him. Instead of being a distant God and unapproachable, Jehovah was interested in the well-being of His children and a provider of all their needs. He was a protector and a defender when they faced their enemies. He was ever-present and all-sufficient. The entire nature of God was love, not terror.

Why is this important? Our view of God and how we live our lives stems from our homes of origin. Our relationship with our parents impacts how we live our lives and affects the way we eventually raise our children, or if we have children. How many children live in *phobos* (terror or fear) of their dad and mom instead of love, respect, and honor? When we have unhealed wounds of fear, we have not been made perfect, complete, and mature in unconditional love (Greek word *agape*).

Fear prevents us from being able to love authentically and from our hearts. Our personal fear blocks us from portraying God's unconditional love to others. Our wounds influence our mindsets and beliefs, and our fear causes us to see through cracked, fearful lenses, preventing us from engaging with authentic love towards others. This creates ungodly mindsets that others are going to hurt or reject us. It is the unconditional love of God that casts out fear from our minds and emotions. The word *ballo* was a root word that was also used in Acts 27, describing when Paul was in the storm and the sailors threw their goods into the sea. The word there was *ekballo* which means a throwing out, casting overboard, or to jettison. God wants us to throw fear out, cast it overboard, and jettison it once and for all from our lives! We need to get ruthless with fear and replace it with God's love.

The unconditional love of God can set our families free. How many families live in fear and not love? Could our faulty views of God Himself form a fear-based acceptance relationship with our children? When parents raise their children in fear, children are afraid to make mistakes in life. They hold back in fear of making mistakes. Fear can become so ingrained that parents treat mistakes as a cardinal sin in the family. It makes children second guess their decision-making ability. When fear is displaced in the lives of parents, it changes the family dynamics for the good and children can rise in healthy, Godly confidence. When the father and mother carry fear into their homes, it subtly shapes and influences the children to carry fear, staying spiritually stunted.

When a father is rooted and grounded in the unconditional love of God, he brings great security to the family. He can protect, provide, and act as a spiritual intercessor in his home. When that role is lived out healthily, his children respond in great security towards him. They will live in confidence knowing that they are securely loved and that they can trust their father. His relationship with his spouse will be secure, as she will trust him. There will always be challenges in the family dynamic, but the family dynamic will remain secure. A man has a responsibility before the Lord to lead his family in love and to lay down selflessly for the good of all in the family. When a man abdicates that responsibility, home-life is disrupted, and confusion enters.

What happens when a man forfeits his authority to lead in love in his home or marriage? The home moves out of God's peace. A spiritual void is left, and his spouse will run the home. Many men are afraid to get counselling and assistance, as they view it as a weakness. Counseling is a form of strength and humility. Many women wish their husbands would heal from their wounds. When men live and love from security, everything flows in God's original design of love.

Men, I implore you to find the heart of God for your family. Get any help you need. Seek emotional wholeness for your family's sake. Counseling is not a sign of weakness. It is a sign you want God's help to become everything He has called you to be. When you can demonstrate the authentic love of God to your family, it will change the dynamics of your relationships in your family and your relationships with others. You were never meant to be a tyrant dominating and controlling your relationships; you were meant to be the servant to your family, laying your life down for your family, as Christ laid His life down for the Church. Paul the Apostle writes, "Husbands, love your wives, as Christ loved the church and gave himself up for her" to the church in Ephesus. (Ephesians 5:25, ESV) When we are emotionally secure, a tremendous amount of security will enter the family dynamic and authentic, genuine love will flow. Men, we have a God-given responsibility to set the spiritual temperature for our households. Do not leave that responsibility to your wife. If we remain stunted and locked up emotionally, we cannot give the love our family needs.

Likewise, when a woman feels insecure, she will grow anxious in her life. Her lack of love and trust for her family and her husband causes resentment and isolation. The supernatural position for a wife is to be in a place of rest and security with God's sovereign leadership, even in her submission to her husband. When a woman is secure in love, she will naturally nurture the family. She will feel safe in her relationships and communicate honestly. She will feel emotionally secure and not go looking for counterfeit affections. She will not be judgmental or try to fault-find her man. It will be an intimate, trusting relationship for both parties. True, authentic communication can flow over a bridge of trust and both parties will find a mutual submission in love towards each other, creating a healthy family dynamic.

God's nature has been unconditional love from the beginning. He continually woos us back to our relationship with Him. When we are made complete and mature in His love, we can be fully free, intimately known by Him, and each other. His love exudes through our being. There is no need to hide anything from God, as there will be an awareness that we are fully known by Him. Though we may view ourselves as imperfect, feeling vulnerable, His love wraps around us like a finely fitted cloak. It is this love that makes us complete and we find rest for a striving orphan heart. The sonship envelops us through love, easily flows in a sweet union between created and Creator. We will not be prone to the suffering of rejection, shame, or assume false identities. We live in great security, free from fear in our lives as we can reflect the pure love of God to others, just as we have received it ourselves.

All You Need is Love

John the Apostle expresses the love of God this way, "we love because he first loved us." (1 John 4:19, ESV) It is God's initiative of love that pursues us. Jesus is the Lamb of God slain before the foundation of the world. God knew humans would fall into fear. Theologically, this is known as divine foreknowledge. Although it is unknown who John was writing to when he wrote First John, it is widely accepted that he is writing to several Greek congregations. His emphasis on the love of God would have helped the Greek congregations relate to God as a loving, intimate Father. It would challenge the Greek culture views on God and their relationship with Him.

The revelation of the love of God is the powerful antidote for fear. When we live out of His love revelation, every relationship we have adjusts. Great security and trust will be formed with people, as fear is dispelled. Authenticity, trust, and faith replace fear and suspicion. Love flows freely. Fear is powerless to stand in the presence of authentic love. True, authentic love is confident and bold. The God kind of love dismantles every argument that exalts itself against it.

Jesus' mission was to reveal the Father in human form. He revealed God as the loving Father and His death and resurrection showed the truest expression of love. In the middle of His greatest pain at Calvary, Jesus was able to see past it. He saw us free from the grips of fear and reconciled to His Father. Before the finished work of Calvary, man lived in fear of a punishing God who was looking to get them. After Calvary, the fullness of God's love was revealed to humans. It was not a cruel punishing father that was out to get them counting their sins against them, but a Father who was intimately interested in our lives, bringing us into our true nature. Our true nature is sonship with Him and true authentic fellowship with each other.

It is God's love that desires to reach out to the world around us. When fear seeks to grip lives and keep people captive, love will want to free people from it. We no longer live under the captivity of a fearful master. True authentic love is pure, humble, and kind, not given to torment. It freely lays its agenda down, trusting and believing the best for every party. Love like that is selfless and rare. It triumphs over every argument that rears its head against it. Even when it is rejected, it does not lash out in anger. It always hopes and trusts. Such true, authentic love will expel fear in people's lives permanently. The real question is, can you and will you open your heart up to such an authentic love like that?

Have you ever considered the difference between discipline and punishment? Punishment instills fear and often shaming behavior. It inflicts suffering to the person for their past behavior and desires to change future behavior with the suffering. It makes a person pay for their mistakes and focuses on controlling a person, rather than instructing a person. When punishment and fear rule, the result is that the person will see themselves as bad and live in shame and guilt. Punishment can be reactive. However, discipline is vastly different. Discipline is rooted in the love of God and instills correct behavior. It focuses on future behavior, causing a change of mind. People who have been disciplined in a healthy way, do not feel shameful and fearful. They realize their behavior was bad and choose to improve their behavior out of love and respect for the other person. Discipline helps a person to deal appropriately and proactively with their mistakes and live in Godly confidence, respect, and love towards others.

Paul instructed Timothy, his son in the faith, that "God did not give us a spirit of timidity (of cowardice, of craven and cringing and fawning fear), but {He has given us a spirit} of power and of love and of calm and well-balanced mind and discipline and self-control." (2 Timothy 1:7, AMPC) When someone lives in fear, their mind is chaotic. Fear torments the mind and influences the thought-life relentlessly. Fear causes the mind to go into fight or flight and paranoia, believing everyone is motivated for harm against them. Fear clouds the mind with confusion, preventing us from thinking clearly. When we are made mature and complete in the love of God, our minds come into peace and we will not be given to anxiety or confusion. We do not see everyone as a threat and will have stability in our lives. We will be able to identify and walk out the will of God in our lives with confidence. The love of God fashions a sound mind within, free from any fear. Even if we are bombarded by thoughts of fear, we will be able to identify those thoughts and surrender them to the Lord.

The prophet Isaiah examines this place of peace when he writes, "You keep him in perfect peace whose mind is stayed you because he trusts in you." (Isaiah 26:3, ESV) When we walk in love, we walk in a steady, upright peace and trust that God is a good Father, watching out for our best interests. We will live in a confident expectation of His workings in our lives. The greatest security that we will ever know is that our Heavenly Father has our back and cares about our every need. The more peace, security, and love we walk in, the more fear will be driven out. Fear will have no place to nest in our minds and we will walk with such a confident assurance and love towards others in our lives.

Authentic love produces an authentic identity, and from authentic identity flows authentic sonship. When we have a secure, authentic identity as a child of God, we will no longer be enslaved to fear. Our spirit will testify an internal knowing that we are His, resulting in us having a healthy self-identity, free from fear. This, in turn, cultivates Godly confidence in who we are. We will not be prone to escape reality or given over to fantasy and delusion and confusion. We will enter a peace of mind and self-acceptance overthrowing any self-deprecation, low self-confidence, and low self-worth. It is from unselfish love that we truly find authentic freedom in our lives, free to express genuine love to the world around us. We will realize all we need is the love of God penetrating our hearts and will watch its supernatural and transformational work in and through our lives.

When we live in fear, we live in continuous condemnation and torment, feeling we deserve nothing but punishment. However, when we choose to live in love, we live in faith, victory, and confidence. God is not up in Heaven looking to punish us for our sins. It was Christ who took our punishment for us.

All You Need is Love

Paul the Apostle described it this way to the church in Corinth, "For our sake He made Christ [virtually] to be sin Who knew no sin, so that in and through Him we might become [endued with, viewed as being in, and examples of] the righteousness of God [what we ought to be, approved and acceptable and in right relationship with Him, by His goodness]." (2 Corinthians 5:21, AMPC)

Christ's finished work transforms our entire nature. What incredible love God has, to do this all for us! Our sin separated us from the love of God, now the love of God reached into our world and became that sin, so we could have restored relationship. It was His initiative all along. Adam and Eve ran from His love in fear in the Garden of Eden, but God loved us so much that He initiated this process, so we could live free. What a powerful divine exchange and what powerful reconciliation we have through Christ's finished work! Fear was traded for freedom and love. These truths of love will lead us into the third antidote for fear. The power of praise and worship.

Take a moment right now to invite the love of God to flood your entire person. Perhaps, you have never known the love of God in your own life or you struggle to receive it. Welcome His love to dispel all fear and welcome it to transform your entire being. Ask God for His love to go into every part of your DNA, letting it transform your relationships with others and your relationship with yourself. Let Him show you how much He loves you. Put some good music on that will allow you to rest in His presence and choose to stay there for a while, as it soaks into your being. He will flood your heart with His love if you will allow Him. Let the love of God work its transforming power in your life. Your entire being will undergo a metamorphosis from the inside out.

// The Power of Praise & Worship

Imagine you are back in the days of King Jehoshaphat. You are in the army of Israel and surrounded by your enemies that want to make war with you. Their sole agenda is to annihilate your people off the face of the Earth. You feel outmatched as the enemies greatly outnumber yours. Would you see this as a fearful time? I am assuming like me, you would be afraid unless you knew how powerful Jehovah God was. Would you recall the times He delivered Israel in times past from your lessons from the Torah? Even after that, would you wonder how God would rescue this time?

Then, you hear the most unusual thing. You hear a prophetic utterance coming from an unknown person. As you hear the word of the Lord, your heart starts pounding in your chest. It ignites your heart with confidence. The word reverberates on the inside of you, "Do not fear. This battle is not yours; it is the Lord's. The Lord is with you." What confidence would come from hearing that? Eagerly, you await the King's order to advance on the enemy, as you have been promised that the victory is assured.

When you awake the next morning, you receive a note from the King's messenger. The memo instructs that you and others have been selected to go before the front of the army singing the high praises of God without weapons. I am sure for a second you would be thinking, "Has the king lost his mind? We were promised victory and now he wants to send us defenseless before the army? I didn't sign up for this. What kind of strategy is that? We were promised victory, but by sending us first, we are sure to lose."

However, not wanting to disobey the King's edict, you submit to his orders, and with the group assembled, you start to sing the victorious praises of God, unsure what to expect. As you walk ahead of the army; suddenly, you look up and see the enemies of Israel attacking each other. You wonder how this could be. Then suddenly, after the two armies finish off one army, they turn on each other, completely ignoring you and your group. They completely slaughter each other in front of you. They completely ignore you. Then, the King of Israel and the army show up. All they see is a slain battlefield full of dead men and the plunder for the taking. Now, that is a powerful victory without even firing a shot.

This account in the Old Testament in 2 Chronicles 20 gives us a glimpse of the power of supernatural praise and worship. It reveals what happens in the natural realm when we engage in the spiritual realm. High praise and worship are some of the most powerful and effective weapons of warfare that we carry in our arsenal against fear. It aligns us with God in total dependency on His goodness to act on our behalf. We enter a place of submission that without Him, we cannot succeed. When we are weak, He is strong and fights our battles for us. We must realize we cannot fight the battles against fear alone. Fear is a spiritual force, and we need spiritual weapons to win our battles.

The Hebrew word for worship is *shachah*. When translated, it paints imagery of bowing down in submission or prostrate in homage to. The Greek uses three words that describes worship. *Eusebeo* refers to reverence and respect, either to God or others. Secondly, *proskuneo* is the action to prostrate oneself or to kiss the hand of the superior one. It is described best as submission or showing profound respect. Lastly, *latreuo* describes the act of serving or worshipping God, the act of rendering or performing services to God or to serve for hire.

Seven different words have been used in Hebrew to describe praise. Those words are: *tehillah, hallal, shabach, zamar, yadah, towdah,* and *barak*. Each of these seven words describe unique ways we can approach God. *Tehillah* praise refers to a song of praise. *Hallal* refers to exuberant praise and to look foolish. *Shabach* means to shout, to command, and triumph in praise. *Zamar* means making music with strings. *Yadah* is the extending of hands in thanksgiving and praise. *Towdah* is a thanksgiving offering. *Barak* is kneeling in humble submission or to bring blessing to God.

We worship the Lord because He is worthy of respect and honor. We *hallal* the Lord in great foolishness to our circumstances with exuberant praise. The imagery of *hallel* can be compared to someone attending a sporting event, as they are fans of a certain team. They get so crazy about their team that they will do anything to show their praise to the team. I am sure you have seen those types. If we got that excited for God, can you imagine what it would mean for our lives? Our lives are laid at His feet in sweet surrender to His will, realizing that it is only He that is worthy. As we worship in our circumstances, we focus more on the goodness of God and less on ourselves and our circumstances in life. The act of submission and surrender reveals how much we trust God to act on our behalf and how we trust God to be our answer. When we look to Him, fear flees. Fear loves to torment us and draw us away from God; praise and worship draws us into God's presence. Praise and worship are an act of faith that invites God into the midst of our circumstances.

Remember when King Saul, in the Old Testament, was tormented by a spirit. It was David who played his instruments before the Lord and the tormenting spirit would leave. David's praise led to freedom from fear. Worship and praise draws us into the heart of God in such a way that fear must be dispelled. It is the love of God that woos us into His presence and out of our fear.

When Paul and Silas were in the innermost part of the prison, even after being beaten, they sang songs and hymns. They allowed the supernatural power of God to move on their behalf. Now, that's true power in praise and worship! Their worship did not come from a desire to be rescued; it came from a desire to exalt God. When Paul wrote "Rejoice in the Lord always, again I will say, rejoice," (Philippians 4:4, ESV) he did not write that when everything was smooth sailing. He wrote that letter as a prisoner in a Roman jail. Not exactly the place you might choose to rejoice.

The very aspect of praise and worship is not situational or circumstantial. It rooted in an eternal, heavenly reality of God's immutable nature. Even if God does not change our circumstances or deliver us, we will be able to overcome every circumstance in our minds and hearts. God will bring us into supernatural peace, free from the fear of the circumstances or their outcome. God is ever-present in them, no matter how bleak or difficult they might be. The Christian faith is a rejoicing, singing faith. It is a faith that overcomes the circumstances we face, even if we are not taken out of them immediately. Our view of reality will shift because God promises to be with us during our situations. He brings us tangible peace and joy, instead of fear and torment, while we are in the circumstances that assail us.

The scriptures address the topic of worry frequently. Worry is a form of fear, whether it be perceived as a lack of opportunity, a lack of resources, or any other form of lack. Worry causes us to lose perspective of the ability of God in our situations. When we worry, we tend to exalt our situations over God, who can overrule our situations and change them. We need to cast our cares upon the Lord. The word for cast in the Greek is the word *epirrhipto*. It paints the image of throwing the care on to the Lord like one would throw a saddle on a horse. He has a deep concern towards us. We were never meant to be burdened down by our fears, anxieties, and worries.

Everyone worships someone or something. We either worship God knowing who He is in our circumstances, or we will exalt our circumstances and worship them. If we focus on our circumstances, we will not see God through them. We will grow fearful, anxious, and start to fret that God is holding back from us. If we choose to worship God in our circumstances, we will begin to see how powerful He can be. Our fear starts to displace, as faith begins to fill our hearts. Our worship takes us out of self-deprecation and low self-worth and brings us to the revelation of how deeply we are loved by our Heavenly Father. Our worship secures us in our identity and reminds us of who God is in our circumstances and fixes our eyes on God. By fixing our eyes upon Him, we live fear-free.

Being able to live free from fear allows us to enjoy our lives fully with others in peaceful relationships. True worship of God becomes the focal point of our lives, knowing that He is with us in every situation we face, either positive or negative.

True worship develops a sound mind within us. A sound mind is set on faith and is in true peace during every situation we face. Worship teaches us who God is in our circumstances and reveals our hearts. It humbles us to a place of complete dependence upon God's ability to give us what we need. When our minds are at peace, we have clarity, focus intently, and the walls of fear that have been erected around our hearts will fall. It is incredibly challenging to focus on life's circumstances when fear bombards our minds like a pounding headache. It is the last thing we want to do, but it is the first thing we need to do. A sound mind can rest confidently in the power of God's ability to act and intervene. Yet, at the same time, we can be at peace no matter what happens circumstantially, knowing that God will be present with His peace and is working all things together for a greater purpose. That peace will be a peace that can transcend all our natural understanding. Paul wrote while in a Roman jail that "the peace of God, which surpasses all understanding, will guard your hearts and your minds in Christ Jesus." (Philippians 4:7, ESV) Now, that is true peace. God triumphs over our circumstances and it is through praise and worship that we see His intervention.

Our worship of God is not out of fear and trembling like a cowering whipped puppy dog forced into submission. Worship must come from our hearts, realizing what He has done for us. Otherwise, it is forced and contrived. God is worthy of worship because He is God and because He is the only one worthy of our worship and our affections. Every other affection outside of His love pales in comparison. He continually invites us to walk with Him in our lives. He has always longed for people to have communion with Him. His unconditional love is the invitation. He sent His Son to lay down His life for us to pay the price we could never pay, and bring us back into right standing with Him. It is always God's initiative. Our self-condemning heart will try to make us earn our way back to the Father's Heart to get acceptance. However, God is constantly wooing us back, pointing us to His Son's completed work on Calvary. We did not earn it. No price we could pay would ever be enough. Jesus already paid the ultimate price.

Our praise and worship provides the confidence to face the most difficult, fearful situations that life can throw, while still standing confidently in the victory of faith. Throughout history, martyrs of the Christian faith stood through immense difficulties, trials, and temptations. They testified of God's goodness to the very end to those who handed them over to death. They could have easily succumbed to the situations, pressures, and fears they faced, but refused. At the same time, there are situations that God intervenes in lives and delivers people from situations that seem so hopeless or bleak. He remains faithful in every situation. Out of that awareness, our hearts can truly praise and worship, displacing our fear whether He chooses to deliver and rescue or allows us to lose our lives for His sake. There is a greater purpose in His masterplan and knowing that to be true, draws us into the heart of a good Father who is ever-present in our situations, calming our fears and giving us supernatural peace. The battle is always for our minds! It is our choice to make.

As you complete this chapter, play a song that ministers God's goodness like an old hymn of the faith such as, "Great is Thy Faithfulness,[xv]" or a new song from Bethel Church in Redding, California or Hillsong Church in Sydney, Australia. Perhaps, God will give you an original song that comes from your heart, as you sit in His presence. Let the words and melody wash over you like a hot shower and penetrate to the core of your being. Reflect on times you were in fear and a song rose from your depths, witnessing to you of His power in your midst. Release your emotions to the Lord and let the words echo as a victory cry in your heart today. Take time to journal your thoughts and see what emerges from your spirit. You will not leave the same way.

12

Standing on the Promises

When we face fear, or during times of great challenge, we must anchor to something much larger than ourselves. This anchor must take root in our lives and hold us through them. What is this anchor, you might ask? This anchor is the promises of God. Throughout history, Godly people have found security and peace, while standing on the promises of God. These people found that God's promises were enough for their trials. One such person who attested to this truth was R. Kelso Carter.

Russell Kelso Carter[xvi] was extremely successful in his life. He was an outstanding athlete when he was younger. Not only that, but Carter was also renowned for his teaching tenure at the Pennsylvania Military Academy. He was a professor of chemistry, natural sciences, civil engineering, and mathematics. Carter was also a devoted Christian and the Methodist Holiness camp meetings he attended had a lasting impact on his life. These camp meetings were so profound that he became an ordained minister to top off his list of life accomplishments. He became an accomplished author and publisher and assisted A.B. Simpson, the founder of the Missionary Alliance denomination, to assemble their hymnal.

It was not until Carter faced a trial of faith that the promises of God became real in his life. A few years prior, Carter had penned the words to "Standing on the Promises."[xvii] Around the age of thirty, Carter developed a heart condition. After many attempts to solve the heart condition medically, the doctors could not do anything more for him. It was at that point that Carter turned to God for intervention.

Carter chose to put God first and consecrated the remainder of his life to God's service. From that point forward, the Word of God took root in his life, and Carter determined he would believe God's Word for the healing of his heart. His faith and determination paid off. Within a few months, Carter's heart healed, and his hymn became a personal testimony. The words of the song and his faith became inseparable.

The scriptures have much to say about the power of God's Word. Several words describe the word for "word". The Hebrews understood God to be a speaking God as He spoke the Earth into existence. They used the term *dabar* to describe the Word of the Lord.

The word *dabar* has two applications. First, it refers to the Word God spoke to man. However, the other application refers to the action produced out of the Word the Lord spoke. When God speaks His Word, He also gives the energy behind it to ensure it is fulfilled. *Dabar* is used over 1400 times in the Old Testament.

The New Testament writers used two Greek words, *logos* and *rhema* to describe "word". *Logos* refers to the written Word of God. It refers to a universal divine reason, immanent in nature, which transcends all cultures and all understanding. When scholars describe the Bible, they always describe it as *logos*. Based on that definition, they determine that the Bible is the established truth for every culture and all understanding once for all time.

A *rhema* is an utterance, instant quickening, or a present Word to our spirit from God. It can reveal a truth found in the scriptures, but also can be used to reveal God's specific will in situations we face. Both the *logos* and *rhema* work together to accomplish God's will in and through our lives.

San Francisco pastor Richard Gazowsky teaches that the Spirit of God acts like a search engine we use on the internet. When we type a topic into a search engine, it uses an algorithm to search the topic and finds webpages connected to that topic through a keyword search. This would be an example of the *logos* in action. Opening the specific website is an example of the *rhema* in action. In the same way, the *logos* is the complete will of God revealed on a wide variety of topics. When the Spirit of the Lord wants to highlight a certain topic or a certain promise in the Logos, this is referred as a *rhema*.

In over 300 references, the Bible instructs us not to be afraid. If a parent tells their children something once or twice, they expect the child to believe what they say. If God, who is much more interested than any parent could ever be about their child, says "Fear not" multiple times in the Word, how much more can we believe it?

The scriptures reveal God's nature and the nature of His Word. The prophet Isaiah describes it this way:

"For My thoughts are not your thoughts, neither are your ways My ways, says the Lord. For as the heavens are higher than the earth, so are My ways higher than your ways and My thoughts than your thoughts. For as the rain and snow come down from the heavens, and return not there again, but water the earth and make it bring forth and sprout, that it may give seed to the sower and bread to the eater, So shall My word be that goes forth out of My mouth: it shall not return to Me void [without producing any effect, useless], but it shall accomplish that which I please and purpose, and it shall prosper in the thing for which I sent it." (Isaiah 55:8-11, AMPC)

Furthermore, when the Angel Gabriel was visiting Mary, to describe what to expect when the Christ was to be born stated, "For with God nothing is ever impossible and no word from God shall be without power or impossible of fulfillment." (Luke 1:37, AMPC)

These two examples, along with many others in the scriptures, all lead to the same conclusion. God's Word has power, it can be trusted, and it can and will be fulfilled in our lives. God takes a personal interest in seeing His Word come to pass.

When we consider fear and faith in God's Word, faith comes by us hearing God's Word over our lives. Faith and fear both influence our lives, but we must choose which one we will let rule. If faith rules our hearts and minds, we will enter supernatural peace, our chaotic lives come into order, and we will live victoriously. If fear rules our hearts, our lives will be full of chaos with internal and external turmoil. We will not have peace in our minds and our hearts, and live anxiety ridden. If the Word of God dwells within us, we will live with the peace of God in our hearts. Both work in conjunction with each other, acting as an umpire in our lives.

Have you ever watched a baseball game? In baseball, the umpire is the final authority to make a ruling. Neither fans, nor coaches, nor players on the bench or on the field can overturn the umpire's ruling on a play, even if we do not like the ruling on the field. We might try to overrule the umpire. We might fight over the call with other fans. We might think the umpire was blind. However, the umpire has the final authority to make the call on the play. Likewise, both the peace of God and the Word of God have the final authority in our lives. When those two elements come into play, fear loses its grip on us. They guard us against subtle lies that fear throws at us. Both testify to our true identity as children of God, and nothing can overturn that calling. We are established in a place of great security through these two elements working in our lives.

Anxiety makes us fearful. The root word for "anxious" or "anxiety" in the Greek *merimnao* is described as pulled apart or divided into pieces. Anxiety pulls us apart internally and divides our thinking. Anxiety distracts us from the peace and goodness of God in our lives and takes us away from it. We were never meant to live in a place of anxiety. Anxiety roots itself in fear and prides itself in trying to make something happen that God did not want to happen. Anxiety tries to break down doors and get people to do things for us that God never intended, leading us into striving. When we live in peace, we will be in a trust-based relationship with our Heavenly Father, knowing that He is with us and has our best interests at heart. There is no need for us to prove His Word to others. We will live peaceful, confident lives trusting that God will open and close doors according to His will.

At the same time, anxiety and fear can hold us back from stepping through doors that God has for us. When this happens, opportunities might present themselves to us, but because of fear, anxiety, and low self-confidence, we may never walk through them. The fear and anxiety mask themselves as self-protection. This self-protection robs us of some of the greatest blessings we could ever have, or prevents us from enjoying the abundant life that Jesus promises.

Standing on the Promises

It is our choice to respond in faith to the Word of God over our lives. God will not impose His will upon our lives like a dominant, controlling father. It has the power to drown our fears completely, allowing authentic faith to arise in our hearts. Faith invites us to God's Heart, even when we have been wounded and are fearful. When faith arises in our hearts, peace supernaturally arises. We might be nervous about what the Lord is asking us to do, but faith in God will invite us passed our fears.

There is a song written in 2013 by Hillsong Church Australia called "Oceans".[xviii] "Oceans" was a major hit having spent forty-five weeks at the number one spot in Christian music. It explores us stepping beyond our fears and invites us to ask God to take us where our trust is without borders, while inviting us passed our fears, passed the waves of uncertainty, into a secure, peaceful place with God. We can then explore God's supernatural grace abiding within us no matter where we walk. This is the power of the Word of God in our lives.

In Matthew 14, we read the account of Peter walking on the water in the middle of the storm at Christ's invitation. There have been many who focused on Peter sinking and Jesus having to reach out to save Peter. Peter did not lack faith. He was willing to step out of the boat to experience a new revelation of the sustaining power of Christ's Word. Christ's Word can sustain us through the storms we face. If we keep our eyes upon Him, we will be sustained through situations that can look bleak and hopeless. The storms, winds, and waves all around us may try to capture our attention, but the Word of God will sustain. When Peter began to sink, Jesus extended His arm to grab him. The Greek word for "extend" in that passage is *ekteino*. One application of *ekteino* is the image of an anchor cast into the water. God's arm is never too short and extends like an anchor to us in our fears and storms of life, and will hold us firmly and securely. This beautiful secure image reveals God's intimate involvement in our lives and how He deeply cares for us. His Word has power to invite us out of our comfort zone, sustain us through our fears, and even if we sink, it is enough to extend to that. Either lifting us out of them or holding us amid them. Now, that Word has power and security during storms of fear!

How should we deal with fear in our lives according to His Word? One way we combat fear is having a living, active Word from the Lord. The writer of Hebrews describes the "Word that God speaks is alive and full of power [making it active, operative, energizing, and effective]; it is sharper than any two-edged sword, penetrating to the dividing line of the breath of life (soul) and [the immortal] spirit, and of joints and marrow [of the deepest parts of our nature], exposing and sifting and analyzing and judging the very thoughts and purposes of the heart." (Hebrews 4:12, AMPC)

The author of Hebrews refers to the *logos* of God as living and active. We need a scripture or a personal prophetic word to stand upon when fear attacks us. It is that quickening, living Word of God in our hearts that acts as an offensive weapon against the fear. We use it like a sword not on the defense to protect us, but on the offense to war against the enemy. The Church was never meant to retreat from fear, but it was called to advance against fear. It is out of living by faith in the Word of God that we overcome fear in our lives.

From the dawn of time, satan has always contended for God's Word over people's lives. In Genesis 3, the serpent was described as craftier than any other beast. The serpent intended to get Adam and Eve off God's spoken promises, while focusing on their own ability and nakedness. The words for nakedness and crafty are similar in Hebrew. Where is the correlation being crafty and naked? They do not appear to have anything similar. It is only when we examine the nature of satan that the similarity becomes clear.

Satan already knew he was naked and stripped of his power from the presence of the Lord. Jesus made mention of this in Luke when He told His disciples, "I saw Satan fall like lightning from heaven." (Luke 10:18, ESV)

The pride that entered Lucifer's heart resulted in exalting himself as being co-equal with God. That action resulted in him being banished from Heaven.

Humans were created in God's image. God declared the image of humans to be good and pleasing. According to Psalms 8:5, we were created below the angels. Adam and Eve were oblivious to sin and its effects and given authority to rule the Earth. It was not until satan tempted Eve with the fruit from the tree of the knowledge of good and evil that humans became aware of sin. Satan used the same tool he used against the angels, deception. The deception used in the Garden was to get Adam and Eve to doubt God's Word. Satan knew what God had told Adam and Eve and he schemed to deceive them into their naked condition and bring them into fear. If satan can get us off God's Word and promises, he can entrap us.

To win spiritual battles, we must remain confident in God's Word over our lives. If satan can get us to give up the Word of God, he can lead us down deception's path, causing us to rely on instinct rather than faith. Our fallen instincts will make us do what we think is right in our own eyes without having regard for God, His Word, or others. The deception draws away from the heart of God and His plans, and can lead us into isolation. When/if we are isolated from relationships, satan can shipwreck our lives.

In the Gospels, satan came and tried to tempt Jesus using the Word of God. It was the same strategy he used in the Garden of Eden with Adam and Eve. Satan is very crafty. He will twist and pervert our understanding, or revelation, of the Word to fit his agenda when we are our weakest. Jesus had been fasting for forty days. Though Jesus was fully human, He was still fully God, but weakened in His humanity. Satan came and used scriptures that Jesus would have studied growing up in Mary and Joseph's house, while attending the temple. However, Jesus, having the wisdom and discernment of God within, could differentiate between truth and error and already knew His destiny and mission.

Standing on the Promises

Jesus faced temptation immediately after He was baptized and received the Father's approval from Heaven. Likewise, in our lives, satan goes after our implanted word of destiny. If he can get us to doubt, or even misfocus on what God has said, he can manipulate us out of our destiny and purpose. The temptation usually comes immediately following something God has spoken about our destiny. This same pattern was repeated previously in the Garden. It will repeat in our lives, as well. It is at those times; we must stand strong in faith and confidently upon the Word of God.

Let me give you an example from my life of how satan tried to deceive me and get me off a Word from God.

In the Summer of 2001, I received what I felt was a divine call from God about living in San Francisco, California, which was confirmed many times though numerous people who knew nothing of what God promised me. However, this promise did not manifest immediately. It was between the Summer of 2002 and 2003 that I faced a 'dark night of the soul' experience.

For those who do not understand what I mean by this, I would describe it as a feeling when the tangible presence of God is withdrawn for a season from a person's life. It does not mean that God is not present; however, it is a season where it feels like little spiritual activity is happening. During that time, there are occasions where people get feelings that life is hopeless and meaningless like spiritual darkness has overtaken them, and they cannot rise above the despair or they cannot feel the manifest presence of God.

I have had several seasons like this in my faith walk. But in the Summer of 2002, I found myself slipping into depression. It was in this vulnerable state, I almost fell for a massive deception. I had recently returned from a mountaintop experience in San Francisco where I believed God was going to fulfill promises that I had been believing for. When I returned to my home city, I felt like a cloud of despair came over me. In the coming weeks, attending church services had become increasingly difficult. I was also struggling with my job. Eventually, that job ended and no matter what I tried to do; every work door closed. California was not opening, and the more I tried to pursue California, the more discouraged I got. Nothing seemed to be happening and I became hopeless, and depression started clouding my thinking. I watched many peers enter dating relationships and get married, leaving me to feel very alone. It felt like a spiritual cloud of darkness was enveloping my life, leaving me abandoned by everyone, including God. I erroneously believed God abandoned me in the middle of the storm of my life and that I would never come out of the season.

There was an engaged couple who remained present in my life during this time. They set their wedding date for 2003. He lived in Europe, she lived in my home city. Both saw my ongoing, continuous struggle to get work. It was during this time, he approached me about working with a friend of his who ran a ministry in Europe. However, I struggled with this decision immensely. God had never spoken to me about moving to Europe. I believed that God was inviting me into a divine opportunity in California, not Europe. But there seemed to be no opportunity in California at that time. There was no word from God in my spirit about Europe and I had no supernatural peace about moving there. It is at times when we are in transition and considering major decisions, that we must choose to follow the peace of God and the personal word of God in our hearts, despite what others say to us.

While wrestling with this decision, I realized that the paradigm my friends were in was not congruent with mine. My friends repeatedly poked holes in my thinking and challenged me to examine my own beliefs and mindsets. I was deeply conflicted. My friend was convinced that it was God's will for me to move to Europe. Deep down in my internal being, my spirit was grieved, and I felt no peace. Daily, I struggled to come into agreement with his reasoning. Eventually, I gave into my friend's thinking as he would not relent. His domineering personality had worn me out. A few weeks later, I met the ministry leader at my friend's wedding. He seemed excited about the possibility of me joining his organization. Over the next several weeks, he promised me he would start looking into the work visa and asked me to visit that August to check out the opportunity.

After succumbing to the pressure from my friend and this potential opportunity, I found myself resenting God for giving me the promise about California. I felt betrayed by God thinking that I had not heard from Him in the first place, and felt foolish for even believing that I could trust God with the promise He made me.

Several weeks before I was scheduled to leave, I had a dream. In the dream, there was a flirty European woman at a church service with me. She was trying to push herself onto me to get me to compromise. I had to push this woman away. At the same, I was preaching about a coming revival. While preaching, the people got restless with me and wanted to throw me out, because I was dressed too casually. Suddenly, a California pastor walked into the scene with his family and told me that I was supposed to be in California. Upon waking up the next morning, I ignored the dream. Deep down inside, I knew God had spoken very clearly that any offer in Europe would be nothing more than a flirty offer.

I continued with my plan to go to Europe. The opportunity turned out to be a dead end. There was no substance to the offer. My theological beliefs challenged the ministry director's and he told me that he could not work with me. I was sent back to Canada without an offer. However, while I was on my trip, the pastor and family from California that were in my dream earlier, visited the same area. They contacted me wondering why I was in Europe, telling me that it was not a correct fit for me. Shortly after returning to Canada, I ended up receiving an invite to move to California and work with their church for a season. They were just waiting for the right timing. I had been vindicated and God fulfilled His Word.

Standing on the Promises

Looking back, I have realized that satan knows how to wear us down. He tries to get us to doubt God's Word when we feel at our weakest. He will try to wear us down with hope deferred and send counterfeit offers. His endgame is to distract us from the promise of God when we are about to enter a promotional time. It is at those times we need to stand firm on God's Word, so we do not get sidetracked and fall into fear. It is faith in God's Word that will sustain us through great trials.

When we have been in spiritual battles for long seasons and discouragement or fear start to enter our thoughts, we must choose to continuously pick up our sword, the Word of God, and fight with it. We must not use it against our brother or sister in the Lord, but we can use it to make warfare against the enemy. Paul the Apostle exhorted Timothy, his son in the faith, "This charge I entrust to you, Timothy, my child, in accordance with the prophecies previously made about you, that by them you may wage the good warfare." (1 Timothy 1:18, ESV)

I enjoy studying history. When I read about the end of World War II, I discovered while the allied forces were liberating the nations Nazi Germany had occupied, they had to have faith over fear. During the liberation of Europe, allied forces would read and hear the propaganda that the Nazis broadcasted and left behind. It painted a bleak picture of doom and fear. The victorious forces were falsely told that they were surrounded and that their battle against the Nazi regime was doomed to fail. The armies had to have the confidence of what their superiors had already said to them about the reconnaissance missions. The spies on these missions had already informed the generals that the Nazis were retreating to Germany to make a last stand.

The living and the written Word act in the same manner as the army commander's orders. They help us engage our enemy when he tries to sow fear and doubt against the promises of God. It is at these times we must act as Jesus did and use the Word as a sword against satan's attacks offensively. When we have the Word of the Lord as a weapon, in confidence, we can stand against fear. It guards us against hopelessness and every other attack the enemy throws at us.

We can confidently know what God has already said in and about our situations through the Bible and prophetic words. We can believe God's Word. Our enemy has been defeated! We can press passed the fear he throws at us. We will secure and enforce the victory in our own lives and the lives of others when we choose to stand on the Word of God.

The times that we are living in are extremely challenging and fear grips the hearts of many. To overcome fear, we must go back to the promises in the scriptures and the promises that God has personally made us and stand on them. It is through standing on what God has already said, that we can fight against the fear that has blanketed our nations. When we are clouded over in our thoughts, we must continually remind ourselves of the promises that have been made over our lives. We can protect our thoughts by wearing the helmet of salvation, which will protect our minds and thought life from the arrows of satan's attacks. The battle we face is for our minds and our hearts continuously. But because of the finished work of Jesus at Calvary, we have been given the victory. It is up to us to enforce it in our lives and the lives of others.

Our God is a great strategist. He never leads us by surprise and guides us if we trust Him and His Word. There are many times I have been aware of God's supernatural guidance in my life either warning or advising me through a dream or His Word. Occasionally, I have gone for a job interview knowing the outcome before the interviewer told me. I have had times God would give me a word of instruction that acted as spiritual rebar for situations I would face the very next day. There were also times when God would caution me about purchasing certain items or forewarning that a job was ending. The circumstances I have faced have contributed to my solid faith and trust in God and His Word.

God lives outside of our natural construct of time. There are times when God will give what I call a "pre-seeding" Word to prepare our hearts. When He speaks, He speaks into our now and prepares the soil of our hearts with His thoughts. When He gives us a Word, it invites us into a process and invite of discovery with Him. As we respond by faith to His Word, faith is ignited in our hearts. We will be tested what God has said and as we pass the tests, His Word becomes a proceeding Word, leading us on an adventure of discovery and exploration of His intended purposes. He does not promise us that everything will be perfect, but He does promise that He will complete His purposes in our lives.

Take some time right now to reflect over your life. Invite the Lord to speak to you about the promises in His Word and over your life. Ask Him for fresh prophetic promises you can stand on. Start journaling the promises He gives and welcome Him into your process of trusting Him to fulfill them. Some of them might be years away and some might come to pass in a short time. Faith in God's Word will develop within your spirit, as He reveals Himself to you as a God who intimately loves you and loves to fulfill His Word and promises.

13

One Small Step

On July 20, 1969, Astronaut Neil Armstrong became the first man to walk on the moon. He and the crew of the Apollo 11 mission were the first NASA mission that landed on the moon. Other missions had orbited the moon, but Apollo 11 was going to have the first people walking on its surface. Upon reaching the moon, the astronauts faced the fear of the unknown. No one had ever walked on the moon before and no one knew what to expect. When Armstrong stepped onto the moon, he made his legendary statement: "One small step for man, one giant leap for mankind."[xix] With those legendary words spoken, Neil Armstrong conquered the fear of the unknown, becoming the first person who walked on the moon. Upon Apollo 11's return, NASA sent several missions to the moon over the next few years, culminating in further discoveries.

In the same way, when we choose to face our fears, we may not know where our journey will lead us. We may pioneer this path in our family line. Making the choice to overcome fear takes one brave step and it takes courage to face it. However, we have the promise of the watchful eye of a Good Father who promises to be with us. Likewise, the astronauts had mission control back in Houston Texas, watching their every move.

Am I free of fear? Not at all. I'm still on the potter's wheel and He is still working on my life. My journey has taught me that God is fully trustworthy and is with me.

If you have made it this far, I hope you realize the journey doesn't end on this side of eternity. There are always more and more journeys that God will invite us into. Our battle with fear does not stop just because we have received a measure of healing. Fear is something we will continuously face and the more we learn how to conquer it, the more we will find victory. Will you take the plunge today? Will you respond to the Spirit's wooing?

Fear is not your birthright. You were never meant to live with fear. Rather, you are meant to live as a victorious overcomer in life, enjoying an abundant, joy-filled life regardless of the circumstances that life throws. It is almost like I can hear the applause of Heaven cheering you on as you run your race. Can you hear them? They are that great cloud of witnesses that have gone before you that the Book of Hebrews mentions. Do not give up. You will make it to the finish line in your race.

One Small Step

Perhaps, you do not know how or where to start your healing journey. The best way is simply to invite God into your journey wherever you are. Ask Him to reveal how fear has affected you. He intimately knows every detail and event that has happened in your life. You may seek out professional help from a trusted counselor or psychologist. It will involve deep soul searching. But if you summon the courage to embrace this journey, you will go on a discovery that will exceed your wildest imaginations. You will enter into a whole new dynamic in your relationships with other people and your walk with God. So today, as the ancient Chinese proverb written by philosopher Lao-Tzu states, "A journey of a thousand miles begins with a single step."[xx] I invite you to take one small step.

Bibliography

Chapter 1

[i] Del Hierro, Jude. "More Love, More Power." The Worship Collection (Vol-03), Mercy/Vineyard Publishing (ASCAP) (admin. in North America by Music Services, Inc. obo Vineyard Music USA), 1987, CCLI#: 60661.

[ii] Dekker, Rachelle and Dekker, Ted. *The Girl Behind the Red Rope*. Grand Rapids, Michigan. Revell, a division of Baker Publishing Group. 2019. Print.

Chapter 2

[iii] "Pandemic". *Merriam Webster since 1828*. www.merriam-webster.com/dictionary/pandemic. (Accessed 19 November 2020).

Chapter 3

[iv] "Casualties of the September 11 Attacks". *Wikipedia*. September 2016. www.en.wikipedia.org/wiki/Casualties_of_the_September_11_attacks. (Accessed 19 November 2020).

Chapter 4

[v] The Editors of Encyclopaedia Britannica. "Third Reich". 9 January 2020. www.britannica.com/place/Third-Reich. (Accessed 19 November 2020).

Chapter 5

[vi] Bretherick, Graham. *Healing Life's Hurts: Making Your Anger Work For You.* Oxford, UK. Monarch Books. 2008. Print.

[vii] Bretherick, Graham. *Free to Be Me: Turning Shame into Freedom.* Nashville TN. Elm Hill, a division of HarperCollins Christian Publishing. 2019. Print.

[viii] Bretherick, Graham. *The Fear Shift: Dominated by Fear No More.* Lethbridge, AB. Run Free Ministries. 2014. Print.

Chapter 8

[ix] Wesley, John. *A Plain Account of Christian Perfection* as believed and taught by the Rev. Mr. John Wesley from the year 1725 to the year 1765. William Pine. 1770. Print.

[x] "Lexus LS 400 Commercial". *YouTube*. 6 August 2019. Lexus's first marketing campaign "Balance". www.youtube.com/watch?v=Do-b4m3m_qg.

[xi] Verma, Sudip. "The Relentless Pursuit of Perfection: The Lexus Brand Strategy". *Business 2 Community*. 19 October 2012. www.business2community.com/branding/the-relentless-pursuit-of-perfection-the-lexus-brand-strategy-0307457.

[xii] *Indiana Jones and the Last Crusade.* Director, Steven Spielberg; Producer, Robert Watts; Screenplay, Jeffrey Boam. "Indiana Jones and the Last Crusade." Hollywood, CA. Lucasfilm Ltd. 1989. Production: released by Paramount Pictures.

Chapter 9

[xiii] Kendall, R.T. *Total Forgiveness.* Lake Mary, Florida. Charisma House. 2007. Print.

Chapter 10

[xiv] Faber, Dr. Riemer. "The Apostle and the Poet: Paul and Aratus". *Spindle Works*. 8 February 2013. www.spindleworks.com/library/rfaber/aratus.htm.

Chapter 11

[xv] Chisholm, Thomas O. "Great is Thy Faithfulness." Language: English, 1923, Copyright: Public Domain.

Chapter 12

[xvi] Carter, Russell Kelso. "R. Kelso Carter, Class of 1867 (Early Graduate)". *Pennsylvania Military College*. 19 November 2020. www.pennsylvaniamilitarycollege.org/r-kelso-carter-class-1867-early-graduate/.

[xvii] Carter, Russell Kelso. "The Story Behind the Song- Standing on the Promises". *Honey For Sweetness*. 30 November 2015. www.honeyforsweetnes.wordpress.com/2015/11/30/the-story-behind-the-song-standing-on-the-promises/.

[xviii] Houston, Joel. Crocker, Matt. Lightelm, Salomon. "Oceans" (Where Feet May Fail), Zion, Hillsong Music Publishing (Admin by Capitol CMG Publishing), 2013, www.hillsong.com/lyrics/oceans-where-feet-may-fail/.

Chapter 13

[xix] Armstrong, Neil. "Armstrong's Famous 'One small step' Quote-Explained". *Navy Times*. July 13, 2019. www.navytimes.com/news/your-navy/2019/07/13/armstrongs-famous-one-small-step-quote-explained/.

[xx] Tzu, Lao. "A Journey of a Thousand Miles Begins with a Single Step". *Literary Devices*. Web. 19 Nov. 2020. www.literarydevices.net/a-journey-of-a-thousand-miles-begins-with-a-single-step/.

Manufactured by Amazon.ca
Bolton, ON